BOUNCER

Geoff Thompson

Geoff Thompson was a doorman for nine years and has been a practising martial artist for over twenty. He is presently qualified as an A.B.A.Assn. Boxing Coach, British Amateur Wrestling Association Coach and holds a 4th Dan C.E.K.A., 4th Dan B.C.A., 2nd Dan K.U.G.B., and 1st Dan Modga Kung Fu. Geoff is a former British Weapons Champion, has competed in the U.S.A. and has trained widely in Aikido, Judo, and is qualified to teach Ju-Jitsu. Geoff also teaches trainee bodyguards his own form of protection on Excel Bodyguard Training Camps.

Also by the same author:-

Watch My Back - *A Bouncer's Story*

The Pavement Arena

Real Self Defence

Real Grappling

Real Punching

and forthcoming titles :-

Real Kicking

Fear - the Friend of Exceptional People

On The Door - further adventures of a bouncer

BOUNCER

Geoff Thompson

SUMMERSDALE

Available from:

Summersdale Publishers
PO Box 49
Chichester
West Sussex
PO19 2FJ
United Kingdom

A CIP catalogue record for this book is available from the British Library.

Printed and bound in Great Britain by Biddles Ltd., Guildford and King's Lynn.

ISBN 1 873475 04 7

The names of some of the people and places in this book have been changed to protect the guilty.

Dedications

I would like to dedicate this book to my late friend and fellow gentleman doorman, Noel Darcy, who paid the ultimate price. He was much loved and admired by many. Also to his lovely mother and father Cathleen and Seanie for graciously allowing me to tell his story and to Noel's brothers and sisters: Maria, Jennie, Laurie, Jacqui, Jerry, Jamie, Paul and Shaun by whom he is sadly missed.

Also, as always, to my beautiful Sharon.

Acknowledgements

To my good mate Alan Bardsley for taking so much time out and helping me so very much (and giving me the odd constructive bollocking).

To John 'Awesome Anderson' whose invaluable teaching still stays with me.

John Jonston, my teacher in the way.

Jacinta, for all her hard work.

To Paul Clifton, editor of 'Combat Magazine' for being so pivotal in putting me where I am today. Thanks, Paul.

To Gus and Tracy, for their continual friendship (and use of the photocopier).

To Ged and Paul Moran for so much encouragement.

To Peter Consterdine for his friendship.

To Ian McCranor for always believing in me.

To Compton for his help and friendship.

To my good friend Rob (Radio Rental) Jones for the original title idea of 'Watch My Back'.

To Peter C., Andy D. (mad marine), Jim Brown and Peter M. Thanks for making me and my family welcome on Excel Bodyguard Courses.

To Dave Turton who is always at the end of the phone line when I need to know something.

Violence

You can run, but it will catch you,
You can hide, but it will seek.
You can close your eyes, but when they open it will still be
there,
You can succumb, but then it will devour,
You can cry, but it thrives on tears.
WARNING! WARNING! Violence is now off the reservation.
Don't run,
Don't hide,
Nor close your eyes,
Do not succumb,
Nor shed tears,
Straighten your spine,
Fix your gaze,
And fight back...then, and only then, are you in with a chance.

G.M.T.

Contents

Preface   8

Foreword   8

1. Choosing   10

2. A Hunt For Gold   34

3. Face To Face With Death   73

4. Three Card Bluff   100

5. Money For Old Rope   115

6. 'Pigs' In The Middle   134

7. Main En Main   139

8. Love On The Door   149

9. Instant Karma   156

10. Retribution   164

11. Robbery At B's   172

12. Death On The Door   182

13. Part Time Soldier and other humorous encounters.   192

Epilogue   204

Preface

"How's work, Ian?" I asked a policeman friend of mine, who was also one of the better students at my Karate class.
He frowned,
"Oh busy, really busy."
"As a copper in Coventry, Ian," I sympathised, "you're always going to be busy."
He feigned a smile, then sighed a deep, 'disappointed' sigh.
"Yea, what a shit hole this has turned out to be!"

Foreword

After writing 'Watch My Back', and recalling some of the happenings of my life, I cupboarded the manuscript, mainly due to laziness and lack of direction, for a couple of years. After the said two years, I gave it a dusting-down and sent the proposed book to my local paper, 'The Coventry Evening Telegraph', for a professional view. I wasn't sure if it was any good or not. Also an article in the newspaper about myself and the book, I thought, might help me to attract a publisher.

After a couple of weeks, Sue Lary, a lovely reporter from the paper, arranged a meet. Joy of joys, she liked the book and agreed to do an article in the newspaper. She also, on my instruction, gave me some very constructive criticism and advice. The floodgates opened.

I took home what was to be the skeleton of my new book, rewriting it completely with extra stories and added description, doubling its contents. However, in the gap between first writing 'Watch My Back', and completion of its publication, I not only remembered many more situations, incidents and altercations, but many more had occurred in the time lapse formerly mentioned. So why not, I thought, write a sequel. Here it is, I hope you enjoy it.

I would like to add at this point that I am not a thug, I have never liked violence and never looked for trouble, though it has followed me around somewhat.

I spend my days trying to be a better person. I ask here as I did at the beginning of 'Watch My Back' that you read with an open mind. If you ever get to meet me you will be surprised, for I am not the person depicted herein. Rather I am a soft, unopposing lover of mankind and all who sail within her. The person herein, my alter ego, is my protector, the person I 'switch on' when the situation demands, these days that is very rare.

Some of the incidents in this book are new, some are old, they are written in the sequence in which I remember them as opposed to the sequence in which they happened, the reason for this is I am forever remembering or indeed being reminded of old incidents whilst at the same time and in the meantime new incidents are happening to me.

To my critics I would ask but one small favour (just fuck off! Only joking) put yourself in my position and tell me that you would have done any less if you were defending the life of your loved ones, don't talk to me about 'sour tasting fruit' when you haven't even bothered to taste it for yourself, and if you still feel that I have 'sinned' then let he who has not cast the first stone.

1. Choosing

In my time as a doorman I have, sadly, seen the demise of many marriages (my own included). Often when the demands of the job get too much it has a direct affect on the family unit: late nights, mood swings, arguments, pent up anger, unutilised adrenaline all add to the toll 'the door' can take. The consequential marital pressure can be devastating. The money? What little there is in the job rarely compensates. Eventually the lady gives her man the ultimatum, 'me or the job'. Some, seeing the light, rightly give up the job to save the relationship, others do not. The choice, of course, is a personal one with many attached contributing factors, each taken on its own merit.

Tony had 'worked' the door most of his life and was married to a lovely girl, Betty, who had bore him beautiful children, but the door was killing what they had and she had given Tony the choice on more than one occasion. This time, though, she meant it. Tony had a very big decision to make: if it were just an ordinary job it would have been an easy decision, but the door is no ordinary job. It sucks you in like a black hole and holds you like metal to magnet. Breaking away, even when you want to, can be a very arduous task. Also your work mates are no ordinary work mates, they are comrades, brothers in arms. The glue bonded affinity is something akin to love, it can get so close that you start wanting to be with them more than your actual spouse, she of course senses this and begins to feel unwanted, second best. The wife of a fellow doormen told him straight,
    "I'm second best to your job!"
    "No you're not," he replied, rather unchristianly. "You're third, I've got a dog as well."

This is where the problems usually start. As a doorman who has perhaps been in a long term relationship, you quite often experience this, due to partner over exposure and the arrival of other interested female admirers who appear nice just because they're 'new'. The beauty at home is very often veiled by the curtain of familiarity. Basically people fail to see what they've got until they lose it, they make the wrong choice, feeling that they 'don't need her any more', then, realising their mistake (this realisation usually occurs when other men start sniffing around) they try to get her back, often though this can be too late, due to the enforced break she realises that she doesn't want him and finds that she doesn't need him quite as much as she thought she did. (Coincidentally this realisation also tends to occur when 'other men start sniffing around'.)

We'd been brought to the 'N' door to clean the place up, like latter day marshals. The place was an infestation of violence, with many of the previous doormen stabbed, slashed, bottled, glassed and threatened with guns (and that's just by the bar staff), the instigators being the scourge of the Bell Green boys, who ruled this area absolutely.

I personally thought little of them, and was more than prepared for the right money to meet them on their own turf. As it turned out the young 'Bell Green' gave me a wide berth and never used or abused the establishment whilst I was in authority there. It was the older ones, who should really have known better, who decided to 'chance their arms'.

First Mr C (detailed account of the Mr C saga in 'Watch My Back') who never got past the first hurdle, then the bullies from The 'O', up the road, who it seemed, thought they ruled the proverbial roost; too many chiefs and not enough Indians it would seem! The 'O' Crew were not kids, they were grown men and fearsome men at that. They had heard that I was coming to the 'N', and I guess they resented me putting my pitch on their park. Quite frankly though, I didn't give a monkey's fuck what they thought. I didn't want trouble with them nor was I about to court it, that was never my way, but on the other hand, I would not tolerate them 'fucking around' in the 'N' whilst I was being paid to protect the place from their ilk.

The previous doormen, I was reliably informed, danced to whatever tune The 'O' Crew played and lived in absolute fear of them, though this was not unusual in this blot area on the Coventry map. The 'O' Crew had gained respect in the city, but it was respect born through the womb of fear, stolen not given. Respect is worthless unless it's earned. Any half-wit can point the barrel of violence at society and 'demand' respect and indeed get it, but the respect only remains as long as the barrel is being pointed, respect of this kind grows a huge nettled by-product, the wart on the lip of humanity, 'HATE'. Real respect, the kind that is earned, brings with it love, warmth, admiration and loyalty. These words lay forlorn, unused or erased from the dictionary of life's bullies.

Saturday night saw me semi-reclined on a cheap white plastic garden chair, my feet resting wearily on the chair in front, half a lager and a bag of smokey bacon crisps at my side, the warm, evening, July sun going down at my front (ah bliss) the 'N' pub entrance to my immediate right and rear. Things were going well and looking good. I'd fought off the attack on my fort by the fearsome Mr C, with comparative ease and though he'd threatened, through the grapevine, to have me shot, (his threats empty it would seem), I was comfortable in the fact that I had made my mark on one of the bigger fish of the manor and that the subsequent ripples would warn off any 'minnows' with a taste for conflict.

"You've got a good job, you 'ave." The unsolicited voice of a local broke my thoughts. I smiled, but never answered. They all say that, but when it 'kicks off' they don't think it's such a good number.

Tony was inside talking to a young lad and a peppering of people sat around the newly refurbished lounge, the room had a bit of a cold unwelcome feel to it like an empty house. Eight-thirty p.m., any time now the place would start to fill up.

I hated it here. I tried to tell myself that it would get better, but I knew it wouldn't. I wasn't comfortable. I'd moved from a lovely, little number in the 'Dip' (Diplomat), to the 'N' because I needed the extra money. They'd smartened the place up quite nicely, but you can't polish a turd, and anyway a bit of paint and wall paper wasn't going to make any difference in this area, it's people that make slums. I had, though, made a lot of friends in the locals who, I think, saw me as their knight in shining armour, who was going to slay the fire-breathing dragons of the manor.

Tony was still talking to the young lad by the bar, when he was rudely interrupted by the tall, lean figure and dark features of a hard faced, black moustached man to his left, who by his drab attire looked in dire need of a fashion transplant. His dark features put me in mind of a Mafioso soldier, his dark marble eyes held a look of malice and sheer nastiness, he was hated by the locals because of his bullying ways. Shadowing him was a giant of a man with a stony diarrhoea-inducing stare that had most people 'shitting themselves' at fifty yards, when this man said it was Sunday, it was fucking Sunday. His gait was totally uncompromising, weighing in at about sixteen stone, he looked harder than a bit of unquarried granite.

Tony didn't know it at the time, but these were two of the leaders of The 'O' Crew, brave with drink and ready to show us who and what they were, though it took the agent of alcohol in their blood to summon the courage. I didn't like either of them, nor what they stood for, one thing was for sure, Karma was chasing at their heels, and it looked as though it had caught up with them in the lounge of the 'N'.

The onlookers murmured in quietened expectation, stomachs churning. They'd seen this movie before.

"Why are you such a big-headed wanker?" The Mafioso's mouth contorted into a make-over of hate and contempt as he asked Tony the loaded question. Bearing in mind that Tony never knew the man, I thought the question a 'tadge' impolite, still, it was asked. Tony's eyes widened: he looked dumbfounded, amazed. He quickly tried to collect himself, he had been hit by a ninety miles an hour 'WOW factor'. Adrenaline comes in many ways, this being the most dangerous because it hits you so quickly that you have very little time to control it. If you see a fight coming you can mentally prepare yourself for the 'adrenal rush' but, if you're not prepared for it and it blindsides you, before you can say 'WOW' it's got you, the reasoning process mistakes the feeling of adrenaline for fear and you're frozen in the face of ensuing danger.

"What?" Tony replied, his face shuddering with the rush of fear and desperately trying to find control. This is the second that all fighters dread, the absolute last second before battle when you know it's gonna go and you want to be any where in the world but where it's at, when you feel like dying, when you want to cry for your mother, when you want to throw up and your legs shake like an agitated conifer, your mouth dries up like you're sucking Clacton sand, your ears blank out everything but the voice of the antagonist, your eyes tunnel like a blinkered race horse and every doubt about your ability to 'handle it' bombards your mind like a jammed switch board, suddenly everything that you romanticised about fighting melts like heated butter and nausea is but a thought away.

'BANG!' It was too late, the Mafioso fired a head butt into his face. Tony, more than a little stunned, grabbed his attacker around the neck, pulled him close and bit a hole in his face (Tony was like that). The shadowy man of stone, seeing his dilemma, joined in on the attack in a bid to help his friend.

"GEOFF!" The loud shout made me jump out of the complacency of my daydreams. "Are you working tonight, or what? Tony's getting battered in there."

It was Gez, my bespectacled friend whose nose was bigger than a huge pile of big things. I leapt from the seat of plastic sending it tumbling to the ground and ran in to Tony's aid. The two men were swinging off his neck, like winter scarves. As soon as I clapped eyes on them I knew who they were, what they were and what was going on. This was an attempt at stamping their authority and letting us know that they ruled the roost. They could find no legitimate excuse for fighting with us, so plied with drink they'd started for nothing, no different really to sorting out pecking order in the school play ground, work place, or the local. In politics, even in marriage, there is an initial battle to sort out who is the boss. I felt nervous apprehension as I approached, in slow motion, (well, it seemed like it) the battling trio. I knew Tony and I were about to destroy these offscourings, but I also knew that it was going to start a war, they were heavy and had been known to introduce 'lead' on more than one occasion. R, the moustached, pit-faced one, was the younger brother of one of Coventry's most famous fighters, and didn't he tear the arse out of it. Everywhere he went, every fight he fought:

"Do you know who my brother is?" or, "I'll bring my brother down here." His brother was heavy, was hard, but that didn't give R the right to go around beating people up or intimidating them in his brother's name, his brother won't always be there . . . he wasn't there tonight.

I'd heard many, many stories of the fighting prowess of his brother Baz, but I didn't care. I didn't doubt the validity of these stories, I knew he was as they said, but I also knew that he was a fair person, a gentleman, and wouldn't go fighting his brother's battles if indeed his brother was 'out of order'.

Tony was struggling to fight off his assailants so I reached up and grabbed 'Stone-face' by the shoulder pulling him free from Tony. As I did so, he turned and threw his right fist in the general direction of my nose, lack of speed betrayed him and I quickly pulled his left shoulder with my right hand forcing his face into three, fierce left uppercuts, the sound of knuckle on face echoing in the smoke filled air, he was in Dreamsville. As he lay helpless at my feet several boots from the crowd that had now gathered around us, shot into his unresponding body with resounding grunts and thuds, the sounds of violence, of splitting skin and breaking bones were sickening. Stoneface had always been an instrument of pain to these amicable locals, the disembodied kicks lay recompense for this. I looked across just in time to see a bloody R scuttling, cravenly out of the exit door, leaving his mate at our mercy, Tony had disappeared behind the bar. I turned to see 'Stone-face' rising bewildered from his bed on the dance floor. Everyone moved away from him, still scared. I lined him up with a right to take him out again: he was by reputation a very 'handy' chap, so I could afford him no chances.

"You've got to leave mate," I told him, the adrenaline pushing an embarrassing shake into my voice. He nodded his assent, at the same time his eyes searched the room for R. I admired him for not wanting to leave without first checking his whereabouts and safety, obviously not knowing that R had 'ran' out without thinking of his safety. 'United they stand, divided they fall'.

"You've got to leave." This time I took in a deep breath to steady my voice and add a little more authority. He stared at me and for just a second I thought I saw a glint of fight left in his eyes, but I guess it was just a piece of shit off the dance floor, because he turned and began to leave.

Just as we got to the door and he was about to go I felt a rush of wind 'whoosh' past my head (fucking beans).

'BANG!' Tony was behind me and let fly with all of his might walloping a huge baseball bat (Karma in disguise) into the back of 'Stone-face's' head emitting a sickly hollow sound and forcing the whole of his body to lurch forward. The connection of bat on skull sounding like a fourteen pound sledgehammer hitting a paving slab. (I can't be sure but I think Tony was annoyed.) My eyes shot around to see the 'out of control', angry, crazy look on Tony's face as he swung the bat again and again at the, now understandably, cowering man before him, who refused to fall over. He did manage to scramble outside but with Tony close on his trail and me close on his. As Tony leathered his fourth shot into the body of 'Stone-face', I thought it about time I intervened to stop the slaughter. I jumped on Tony's back, unfortunately just as he was retracting the bat for his fifth home run and the offending wooden implement whacked me on the head. I held him tightly around the neck to try and stop him destroying 'Stone-face' but, Tony being twenty stone and me being a mere lightweight at thirteen stone, he threw me around like a flag. I was just like a jumper on a windy clothes line.

After what seemed like a life time of 'flying the flag', I finally managed to stop the onslaught, probably saving 'Stone-face's' life (and he never thanked me, you know). As Tony went back inside 'Stone-face' hobbled off in the general direction of The 'O', holding onto his head like it was about to fall off, (I think it was) he didn't look quite so menacing now, in fact he looked rather pitiful.

Tony was still going crazy. He shouted,

"Where's the other wanker, the one who nutted me?" (He was still annoyed, I could tell), then ran, still wielding the bat through the lounge and into the toilet in hot pursuit of Rob. I ran after him again to make sure he didn't do too much damage. The communal troughs lay empty.

'Thank fuck for that', I thought. One of the two cubicles, though, was locked, obviously occupied. Tony kicked open the cubicle to reveal a skinny, trembling, bespectacled man sat on the toilet with his trousers around his ankles, who had just found an immediate cure for constipation in the form of a twenty stone, baseball bat proffering madman (a close encounter of the turd kind). He wasn't 'our man', (I was glad, it would have been a messy 'job') so we closed the broken door and went back to the lounge, where I finally managed to calm Tony down.

V, the shirt and tied manager with specs and a round, soft face, shakingly approached us.

"Do you know who they were?" We both looked at him. I knew, though it was obvious that Tony didn't, because when V told him, he went pale. He knew it meant war as well. V, I've got to say, was a spineless bastard who didn't even have the dignity to try and hide his sheer and absolute panic. The trouble with panic is, when openly displayed, it becomes highly contagious, and everyone in close proximity to 'whimpering V' seemed to be coming down with it, and running around in a frenzy. I kept myself calm, though I could feel the extreme strain of panic trying to crack my will. I fought against it with the army of my self control. I said very little.

"They'll be back," everyone kept telling me. "Get out of it Geoff, they're too heavy". All trying to worry-monger me, but I wasn't having any of it. I carefully picked my words in answer to their statements.

"Let them come, I'm not going anywhere." I wanted to, though. I wanted to go home, far away from it all. I wished it hadn't happened, and that I wasn't involved but I was and it had happened, so I might as well get on with the job in hand, I told myself. In this job you learnt all about fear, you also learnt to expect its company. This was the third and most corrosive form of adrenaline, probably the one that slayed more doormen than any of the other forms of adrenaline, mostly due to its absolute unexpectedness. This is the adrenaline of aftermath, win or lose this 'will' executioner would arrive and flood you with the chemical adrenaline that would gnaw away at you and fill you with negativeness and worry. This feeling is also catalysed by 'people' who feel it their job (so nice of them) to remind you constantly of the dilemma that you face. The key with this baby is expectancy, after every battle I mentally prepare myself for its arrival, if you expect a blow then its impetus is greatly lost, though it is still a bastard. I've witnessed the demise of more doormen due to the phenomenon of adrenaline aftermath than any other reason.

"Do you think I was over the top, Geoff? With the bat I mean." Tony's voice sounded shaky, his face held a worried hue. He didn't want to be here, either. I was blunt.

"Yea, you were over the top, Tony. But don't worry about it because it's done. There's nothing we can do about it now."

Tony and I were on our own. Two other doormen that worked with us didn't want to know, it was all too much for them. That was their prerogative. I just hoped that they didn't stand in what they were made of on their way out the door. You don't mind people losing their bottle, you even understand it, there is a very thin line between being a hero and a coward, in fact it boils down to a single decision, stay or go? It's just the fact that it leaves you in such a shit mess, still at least you find out who's who. Trouble on the door is, as I see it, a character pressure test, some get through it, others don't.

V was still running around like a headless chicken, spouting about how we were all doomed. Excited, frightened chatter had spread through the room like a plague, it was also emptying by the minute.

Then the aftermath catalysts began their work.

Every which way I turned somebody seemed to want to tell me what grave danger I was in, trying to worry-monger me, frighten me off, dying to see the arse fall out of my trousers. I stuck to my one-liner and told everyone the same thing.

"If they want to fight, I'm here. They can come, I'm going nowhere."

I'm always careful of what I say and how I act when the heat is on, because when it's all over every single word will be remembered, recalled and recounted like previous convictions in a court room. Better to be remembered for strong words than weak ones.

A huge fat, bearded man with more chins than a Chinese telephone book, who must have got his underpants on prescription, walked past me on his way to the exit. He stopped briefly by me (as they do) and whispered,

"There are thirty of them on the way down, and they've got guns." A rush of adrenaline shot through my body as he spoke, I fought to control it, but it was running riot. I hid it, never let it show. You can't show any weakness, got to hide them.

"Fuck this," said Tony. (He had a way with words.)

"Shut the doors, shut the doors," shouted V hysterically.

Somebody locked the front doors. Tony picked up his baseball bat from behind the bar where he had left it in a bucket of cold water to cool down. I relieved my laden pocket of the 'steel fist' therein contained. Tony looked at the steel and smiled, I smiled back,

"Fancy finding that in my pocket."

I put my mind into top gear, when they crashed down the door I was going to hit anything that moved, fight till I dropped, anyone who touched me was going to 'have some'. I might well lose, I surmised, but I was going to take teeth and flesh with me. If these people wanted to dance, I thought, then play the music and let's do it. With the doors closed the room now seemed darker and morbid with silhouetted figures standing and sitting all around. A hum of anticipation hovered in the room like a bad smell, I heard shouting from outside, much shouting, Tony's face gave an involuntary shiver and his eyes locked on to the space by the front door. He gripped the bat so tight that his fists went white (though not as white as my face) and shook the bat as though readying for a fast ball.

We became oblivious to all else in the room. We were locked into combat mode, ready for battle. Nothing and no one else existed. For those few seconds before there seemed to be nothing else in the world but us and the door, the fear had gone now replaced by an acceptance of 'what will be' and in those seconds is found a matting of spirits that sporns camaraderie. If we never ever saw each other again for the rest of our lives this moment will be engraved in our very souls.

'CRASH!' The first window went through, shattering on a large, pregnant woman, forcing a scream from her throat and more screams around the room. 'CRASH! CRASH! CRASH!' All the other windows smashed, spitting glass this way and that. My eyes never left the closed front door for what was an houred second, my fist clenched tightly around the cold steel of my 'duster'.

Amidst the madness I said to Tony,

"I think we've upset them."

He never answered, I never expected him to. My eyes refused to blink, my heart pounding on the cavity of my chest like it was trying to get out, mouth dry and pasty, the smell of fear infiltrating my nasal passage, my legs trembling with the flow of adrenaline. Tony lifted his bat like an axe-man at an oak, in baited anticipation for the crashing in of the doors. This was it, this was the big one. 'CRASH! CRASH!' More exploding windows, still we waited, ready now. The room was a flask of screams and yet it was deathly silent, we were experiencing adrenaline deafness, willing it to happen now, wanting it to happen just to get it over with, no longer giving a fuck, just glad that one way or another it was nearly over. Handling a fight, no matter how violent is a lot easier than handling the possibility of a fight, that monkey on your back is more corrosive than caustic, it reaches a point where confrontation becomes easier than anticipation so you just want to do it and get it over with.

"They've gone!" a disembodied voice shouted, piercing the adrenaline deafness like an arrow. A thousand relieved sighs rolled through the room (nine hundred and ninety-nine of them were mine). But the anxiety remained. I knew that this little episode was only the beginning, it was far from over. I knew, I'd been here before.

V 'the wimp' went straight back into his 'dance of the headless chicken' routine, looking at every broken window as though it was ancient, stained glass and cradling every broken piece as though they were smashed antiques. He moaned and whimpered and I despised him for being so unashamedly blatant about it, not so much because I didn't like cowards, after all we are all cowards just waiting to happen, it was more that I found his weakness unnerving, almost infectious. I told him to 'shut his fucking mouth, it's only glass'. V is the father who asks, when his daughter crashes his car, how much damage has been done to the car, with no concern for the well-being of his off-spring. Thoughtless bastard!

My bed was a vipers nest of sleeplessness. I rolled and re-rolled the night's happenings over and over again in my mind like a favoured film. Studying and analysing, looking at it from every conceivable angle and then again, like a complex equation that demanded an answer, but seemed not to hold one, like searching a pitch black room with your eyes closed for a pin . . . that isn't there. I re-called my decimation of 'Stone-face' and how surprisingly easy it had been. I was non-plussed. His 'rep' as a fighter was big and he'd taken out (and I don't mean to dinner) many fighters that I personally rated. Perhaps his coup-de-grace was due to an off night, or maybe too much beer, perhaps I was lucky (NO WAY!) or was it due to the cripple shooting, awesome power of God, Karma and the law of averages, all catching up on him at once via that ugly hand-maiden, violence, and yours truly, administering the penance of a severe 'caning' followed shortly by unconsciousness, and then by a gutted loss of confidence. Then assisting in his demise still further, a bounce on the head by a twenty stone, raging baseball bat. Definitely not one of 'Stone-face's' better days. Still, what goes around, comes around. The consolation of my victory over 'Stone-face', though, was still not enough to buy me any sleep. Even as I left the pub that evening, I knew that sleep would elude me, it always did in times of high stress, it was a part of the toll that this kind of life exacted. My only real consolation was the fact that I knew I wasn't the only one who would be losing sleep, after all, it wasn't I who had my reputation shimmied all over the 'N' dance floor like a cleaner's mop, nor I who'd thrown the gauntlet with all my might and got a spanking for my troubles. If (I surmised) I was lying on a bed of nettles then they must, surely (don't call me Shirley), be lying on metaphoric hot coals.

The next day phone calls were made, many phone calls. A show of strength was needed (actually a fucking army was needed) but it wasn't a problem, my friends were many and everyone asked would, I knew, come to my aid.

The shimmering, evening sun shone down on the 'N', a large, detached pub that sat on the bank of the Coventry canal, like a moored narrowboat. At the front, it faced onto a busy, main road at the pit of a hump-backed bridge, a mere 'knife's throw' from the infamous Bell Green, where violence was more common than fish and chips, and craft-knifed and Stanleyed faces were in abundance. Severed ears, the result of venomous battles, were worn as 'prizes' on key rings, or if the said 'prize' had been cut or bitten off the head of a 'named' fighter, auctioned in the pubs to the highest bidder. The unfortunates who lost the ears, forever on afterwards, bore the brunt of many unsolicited jokes.

"Can I get you a pint?"
"No thanks, I've got one 'ear!"
Or if just a part of the ear had been lost,
"No thanks, I've got a half 'ear!"

Inside the 'N' the lounge was full to capacity with doormen, forty to fifty all told, with not a weak link amongst them. Everyone could and would go the distance, everyone a rook or a knight or a king, no pawns in this crowd. Every fighter in the room was the 'man' in his own particular area of the city.

Tracy, from Wyken, was short with cropped light hair (courtesy of Winson Green prison), and a hard, scarred face. He was tough and uncompromising, a wizard with a baseball bat.

'Ginger' John, was also small in height, though very large in stature. Diminutively innocent looking face, but held faultless 'hands' and a cast iron will. Nicknamed 'Horlicks' by his fellow doormen, because he always put people to 'sleep' last thing at night.

'No-neck' Maynard, no neck and no heart.

'Awesome' Anderson, who quite simply was.

Ricky 'Jabber' James, the towering seventeen stone Midlands pro-boxing champ, if his opponents lived after he punched them it meant that he'd used 'control'.

'Killer' Kilbane, if his cripple shooting right never put you to sleep, his vignettes of past battles won, would.

Kev, he was a gentleman, but his alter ego issued a psychotic fighter who ruled the unrulable Willenhall with unpretentious certainty.

'Wicked' Winston, whose 'people pummelling' hands etched themselves into the brow and memory of everyone unfortunate to have 'stopped' them.

'Sheffield' Johnny, whose personal armoury of weapons could only be matched by a platoon of Paras. Legend has it that he once tripped and fell, stabbing himself six times.

And more, many more. I was the proud host of the greatest assembled 'team' ever to stand together in one room. The 'O' Crew had met their masters. As always happens when fighters get together, stories and tales of past battles (more exaggerated at each telling) were being bandied around. There were, metaphorically speaking, dead bodies everywhere.

Tony was a big man at twenty stone. He approached me, cigarette in hand, his robust, scarred face (it looked like a map of the London underground), capped by dark and smartly parted short hair, he looked tired and bedraggled. His eyes betrayed him. The pressure, I knew, was getting to him. His hand shook as he lifted the cigarette to his lips and drew heavily upon the weed. He kept an even look on his face, to hide his fear, it was hidden from most, but to me it stood out like a bulldog's bollocks. I hated to see him this way.

"I don't need all this," (tell me about it) he said quietly. "I never slept a fucking wink last night." (Tell me about it again).

He wandered off and made polite conversation with our guests. John 'Awesome' Anderson approached me. He stood straight backed and confident at five foot eight inches, his skin a caramel brown with a thin pencil moustache below a freckled nose and dark, hard eyes, that to the uninitiated looked mean and unwelcoming (and why not, they were). To me, John was a brother.

"Where are they then?" he asked, then slowly drew on his cigarette, his eyes squinting in motion.

I shrugged my shoulders negatively.

It was nine-thirty p.m. and our sparring partners had not yet arrived. We'd had it on good authority that they, The 'O' Crew, had planned a return visit for tonight. They had sent a few spies down to see what kind of firepower we were holding. The returned reports must have put the shits up them, because they never left the safety of The 'O'.

"I'm sick of this fucking waiting," said John. "We'll send a scout party down there to see what's keeping them." John wasn't one to hang around, he'd fought that many battles that the locals had nick name him 'one man gang'.

At this John, Colin, Ricky, Winston, Paul and Big Neil (not one under fifteen stone, collectively they looked like the training camp for the Dallas Cowboys) sauntered off down the road to The 'O' and entered the unwelcoming (understandably) bar of the enemy's pub, brought drinks and sat in the middle of the large bar like lone lambs in a forest of wolves. They were made as welcome as syphilis. The crowded room fell as silent as a funeral parlour, except for the confident banter of 'Kamikaze' John, and the boys who laughed and joked with each other, just to let The 'O' Crew know that they didn't 'give a fuck'. There is nothing more intimidating than walking into an opponent's lair and displaying blatant fearlessness. The 'O' Crew had never experienced such a display of courage, and it scared them, they weren't used to it, they were only used to giving it out, and another thing, they never slept a wink last night either.

V, when he found out that the lads had gone up to The 'O', was, to say the least, not a happy chappy, and he told me so.

"I never told them to go up, they went of their own accord," I told him. I looked closely at this portly, middle aged man and wondered what the hell he was doing in a trade like this, he looked like he would be more suited to managing a supermarket. Basically he was a nice man in the wrong job, the stress must have been taking years off his life, it certainly was mine.

When the lads returned, they were in good spirits, they couldn't believe that these so called hard men had let them, so few in number, in and out of their castle unchallenged.

"Wankers," John, the man of few words concluded. I had to agree, last time The 'O' Crew had trouble, with the doormen before us they had turned up in large numbers with hand guns and made the doormen get on their knees and beg, they didn't seem to keen now that the odds were a little more even.

The rest of the night, not surprisingly, went without incident. If it was going to happen it would have been tonight, I told myself. Of course, the locals said and kept saying 'they'll be back, and soon', and because I was the head doorman and it was my mates that dared to tread on their territory, I was the one that was going to 'suffer'.

"They do house visits you know," A kind, informative, worry-mongering local told me.

"They got one chap in his house, beat up his wife, locked the kids in another room, then pummelled him to fuck. Beat him so much that he pissed and shit himself, spewed blood and was in a coma for ages." (Not the kind of boys you take home to meet mum).

"Is that right?" I said, feigning disconcern, hiding the fear that the words instilled in me. I think that this nondescript, worm of a man was hinting that I was going to get a home visit, and 'hey, don't you have a wife and kids?'

"They can knock my door anytime they like, but the bastards will only do it once." I pointed aggressively at my own chest, "I do home visits as well, and I'm not the only one around here with a wife and kids. Tell them from me that I'm ready when they are!" I threw the words at him like stones from a sling, and he backed away from me. In days of old the bearer of bad news was always killed by the recipients. If he didn't fuck off quick I was going to regress myself back a couple of hundred years and obliterate him. Just another worry-monger trying to crack me, dying to see my weaknesses seep blood like from the fractures of my mental armour. I did indeed harbour weaknesses, and yes they were trying to break out, but I would never, never let them. I had, through training in Karate hardened and reinforced my will with the sturdy steel of stubbornness, wild horses wouldn't pull it out.

Another restless night of tossing and turning lay before me, but I could handle it, stress and I were kin. We ate together, slept together, worked together and trained together. It was an absolute and utter bastard at times, but you learnt to live with it, you had to. It was at times like this that you earned a year's money all at once. For every pound that you earned you paid back double in stress destroyed brain cells. Nagging doubts about my ability to handle this situation were beginning to filter through my resolve, four days and many threats had gone by since the incident. Beautiful cooked dinners were force fed and lay on the lining of my stomach like razor blades. Sex had become an effort, every time I reached the 'vinegar strokes', the aforementioned threats swam, unchecked into my temporarily unsentried mind, reducing the whole performance to lacklustre. I promised myself that this would be the last time (for fighting, not sex) and after it was sorted out I'd 'lose the door' for some job less destroying. I'd pull away from this thing called 'violence', become a recluse.

What a lot of bollocks!, and I knew it.

A few months after it was over, I knew I'd be regaling to my mates, 'the time I cleaned up in the 'N'' (no, not with a mop and bucket). Romanticising the whole shabang to fuck, making out it was all a bit of a wheeze, a little fun. The vignettes totally lacking the cold reality of violence and its 'soul brother' the diarrhoea inducing, FEAR.

Visualisation was a small escape. 'Thud . . . thud . . . thud . . . thud'. My fists sank into the canvass of my punch bag that I had visualised as flesh and bone. In my mind's eye, I watched my antagonists and attackers fall at the mighty wrath of my pain inducing fists. 'Humph, hu-humph.' I cracked my well practised attacking feet into the belly of the bag letting out a chilling, blood-curdling shout,

"KIAAAAA!" (The neighbours must have thought I was killing the cat). I was really there. I felt satisfaction as their bodies fell before and around me, grey with unconsciousness, involuntary shakes running through their cadaver-like bodies, as they hit the pave stones with the cold, sickly wallop of a raw chicken hitting the cutting board. Salty sweat stung as it ran into my eyes from my forehead, my nostrils inflated and deflated like a raging bull, steam rose from my head, my teeth gritted as I sucked in air. I will never give in, NEVER,

'THUD!' My right fist buried itself deep into the punch bag to underline my resolve. I grabbed the bag and bit hard into it like I was tearing off a nose, spit and snot splattering everywhere. The thing with pressure is that it flows over into your private life, everything goes on hold until the situation is resolved, sometimes that can take months, coping with the pressure leaves you little energy to do anything else like play with the kids, you also find yourself short tempered, and who gets it? Those closest to you, you want to ask them for help but there is nothing that they can do, nothing anyone can do, and all the time Mr Negative keeps trying to crack you telling you that 'you can't handle it, you're finished', 'give in', 'everyone will understand'. But you learn from experience not to take any shit from Mr Negative because if you do he fucks you up badly, once you allow him house room he devours you mercilessly, as soon as he comes in to my head I fuck him off straight away, I bash him back with Mr positive, or just ignore him like a sniffy subservient.

Wednesday night again saw me at the front door of the 'N', Alan by my side, my best friend. He wasn't there on the night of the fight, but he was here now. He'd been warned, as had I, that he ought not 'fuck' with these people, but wild horses wouldn't keep him from my side, especially after he'd been warned off. Al was a physical and mental power house.

Nine p.m. and Tony hadn't turned up yet. I half expected him not to turn in at all. He'd had his life threatened as had I, and the pressure on him at home didn't help. He had a choice to make, the door or his family. The choice wasn't quite as simple as it might seem because if he left the job now, in the midst of a crisis it could be seen by others as a bottle drop (only Tony and I would know the real reason) then the reputation he'd spent a life time building would be lost in one fatal swoop, to people like Tony this is like pulling the plug on life, it meant losing everything he believed in, everything that he'd lived for, this is a concept that ordinary people will never understand, but, when you've been a King it's very hard to have to play a Pawn.

To try and resolve the situation I had attempted to set up a 'one on one' between Tony and 'Stone-face'. The message returned to me was negative. I was told that they (The 'O' Crew), didn't want any trouble with me, I was a gentleman, they only wanted Tony. This one statement was showing me their hand and it wasn't a good one. I sent a message back saying that Tony and I were a team, and that they couldn't have one without the other. I was told from other sources that I, being the head doorman and in the unenviable position of 'in charge' was going to have my legs blown off and then my arms (a little bit severe, me thinks). And as if that wasn't enough, on Saturday night we were going to get a visit from the petrol bomb wielding Hell's Angels.

Tony arrived two hours late at ten p.m., there were a few locals enjoying a drink in the lounge, Alan had just nipped to the loo (where all the big nobs hang out). I sat on my favourite, plastic, garden chair outside on the patio, enjoying and savouring a lovely half a lager and a bag of smokey bacon crisps as he approached. He looked surprisingly jolly as he bounced up the three steps and onto the pub's patio, where I sat, thinking, 'What the fuck's he got to be happy about, didn't he know that I'd only got a couple of days left in which still to enjoy my arms and legs?' We exchanged greetings, he apologised for being late, I accepted his apology (we danced). He wasn't really happy, and I guess he'd made his choice, in my opinion the right choice,

"Guess what?" he said, manoeuvring the conversation to the inevitable. "What?" I replied.

"I've got myself a job as a security man."

He had chosen and the moment was a sad one.

"The only trouble is it's shifts," he added. I knew what he was saying, although he never said it out right, he was telling me that he was leaving, that his family were the most important thing in his life and that the door came a very sorry second.

"Great. So what does that mean exactly?" I replied.

His smile evaporated, his eyes dropped. In his big face where I'd once saw strength I now saw sadness, where once was emblazoned unity I now saw confusion. It made me sad, I had always seen Tony as a rock, an island, I knew how he felt because I was feeling the same.

"Look Geoff, I've been doing this job for fifteen years, I've been there, I've seen it all, but now I've had to make a choice. I need my family and I don't need the door. I'm packing it in." He looked up at me and our eyes met (we danced again), I smiled sympathetically. A mixture of relief and sadness ran through me. In a way I was re-lieved that he was leaving because I knew that his leav-ing would put an end to the blood bath that would surely ensue had he not stopped. Tony knew this too, and it was partly why he was leaving. I also felt ashamed at feeling relief/sadness.

To me, Tony leaving the door was an end of an era, he was an institution, untouchable, it shook the very foundations of everything that I believed in. The choice he made was a very brave one, he had chosen his family above all else, and I admired him for that, I knew what leaving the job meant to him, I also knew many men who were not brave enough to make the decision he had.

No-one resented Tony for leaving (V 'the wimp' nearly wet himself with joy), they all respected his decision and understood the pain he must have gone through in reaching it.

Our eyes fixed a long gaze (not another fucking dance!), I reached out and put my arms around his huge solid frame and we hugged, (in a very manly kind of way).

"Just remember, Tony we're brothers and I love ya".

He half smiled,

"I know."

This, of course, was the loop-hole The 'O' were looking for, they wanted a way out that wouldn't lose them too much face. This was it, with Tony gone they had no reason to fight any more. 'Saturday' threats still came our way though, so minus Tony, Alan and I manned the door with a duster (not a feather one) and a bat, not much of a defence against a gun or a petrol bomb I grant you but it was slightly better than nothing.

Saturday night came and went, albeit very slowly, without incident. On the following Tuesday The 'O' Crew came to the 'N' when I wasn't there to call a truce with V, it was granted. Peace and tranquillity came to the forefront once again. The locals were jubilant because the outcome as they, I and everyone else saw it, was a major victory for us.

With the rats of The 'O' led off to the drowning river of humility and defeat by Alan and I with our 'pied pipe' of courage the 'N' manager V didn't want to pay the piper.

Now that the danger had subdued he thought that he could drop wages and lose doormen.

"Well we just can't afford to pay you as much now, Geoff." His whole body shook as he spoke to me, I think he was expecting a dig.

"Hold on a minute V, are you telling me that after all the shit we've been through you're gonna drop our money?"

"It's not exactly like that Geoff, just get rid of a couple of the lads and you can have their money, there's no reason why you need lose out."

I shook my head in disgust:

"Are you not happy with the job we've done, I mean what kind of bloke do you think I am, do you think I'm gonna let people go and have their money, that'd make me a bigger wanker than you V." I pointed at him to add emphasis, he bowed his head down and didn't answer, I shook my head again.

"You should be ashamed of yourself V, you're lucky I don't give you a dig. I tell you what you can do with your job, you can stick it up your arsehole." At this I walked out of the pub.

Two months after I had left, the pub was once again infested with violence, a shit hole full of drugs: if the place had burned down the whole of Coventry would have been high.

Several months later I got to meet R's brother, Baz, socially. He was one of the toughest, most charismatic men I have ever had the pleasure of meeting. He was also, as I had rightly thought, a gentleman.

2. A Hunt For Gold

The rap of brass knocker on the porch door echoed through an empty house. Her stomach clenched with apprehension, no reply. She knocked again and stood back so as to get a full picture of the house, her eyes scanned the bayed, Georgian window, then the bedroom windows for signs of life. The door knocker rattled for the third time, she had to be sure that no-one was at home in this modestly detached, fashioned from brick abode. Her calculating beetle-black eyes again checked all windows for signs of life. Black hair hung lankly above and around her much beaten, etiolated face, stolid from a lifetime of batterings. First from her dad, then from her brothers and now P, who, though villainous, seemed so sweet to her before the wedding that she thought life might be taking a turn for the better. The broken nose he gave her as a wedding present soon put paid to those dreams. Her drab, food-stained attire hung loosely from her emaciated frame, like a man's suit on a broomstick.

The knocked door was answered not. She felt a surge of excitement rush through her body as she walked down the paved entry to the rear garden gate, avoiding the drip, drip of water from the upstairs overflow pipe. The gate, much to her delight, was unlocked. 'Fucking amateurs', she thought, 'won't they ever learn?'

This house was an early Christmas present, a gift from God. Huge conifer trees to the front and rear ensuring seclusion. A neighbouring detached house set slightly forward to the left and a detached house set slightly back to the right. Built that way to ensure privacy for the owners, but a Godsend for thieves and vagabonds. The temerity with which she kicked through the low-level kitchen window was born to two things. Vast experience in burgling houses and the fact that this was the fourth time she'd robbed this particular house. No burglar alarm, no dogs, no nosy neighbours, happy birthday! It was like taking candy from a child.

As the glass shattered into the kitchen, the next-door neighbour's dog barked out an alarm and ran to the 'help the burglar' erected six-foot fence. She tucked herself back in the entry for a moment, just to make sure the dog wasn't followed by an inquiring neighbour. It wasn't. The fucking dog barked so often that they had learnt to ignore it.

There were four locks on this door, only three of which were in operation. The top inside bolt was not secured, the middle key lock was. The switch lock on the door handle was and the lower bolt was. The lower bolt and switch lock were quickly unfastened leaving only the obstacle of the key lock, which was really no obstacle at all because the stupid bastards had left the keys on the window ledge. Here lay her first error; in her haste reach up through the broken window to get the keys and open the last remaining lock, she nicked her arm on the broken glass, causing it to bleed profusely, a heavy clue for a later pursuer. With all locks disarmed, she opened the kitchen door and made her way inside. 'Ah', no wonder it was so easy this time, she could tell by the change in decor, by the new brown kitchen carpet tiles and the general fresh smell that the house was now occupied by a new family. The constant robberies must have driven the last family out and in their haste to sell to the dewy-eyed love birds, whose dream house this obviously was, they neglected to mention the poor history the house, beautiful though it was, held. As though the estate agents might advertise, 'a beautiful, detached three-bedroomed house, in a quiet cul-de-sac, much sought after - by burglars'. I don't think so!

Gold and currency. That was all she took, nothing more, nothing less. She prided herself on this. Televisions, videos, stereos, electrical gear, no good. She only took what she could safely conceal on her person. She was factotum to her inability to drive or, in fact, afford a vehicle if she could. Drawers and cupboards were carefully checked, her eyes danced around every crevice in the room, her fervour was almost palpable. She tensed her rectum as her churning stomach tried excitedly to push out last night's curry. She knew this feeling well and that it would ebb as she became more familiar with her surroundings. A trickle of blood dropped from her arm, so she wrapped a kitchen towel around the wound and continued her search. She was a gentleman burglar, if there is such a thing, in that she left everything relatively tidy and never, like many burglars, emptied her bowels on the carpet and the furniture when the urge took her.

She was familiar with the type of electric cooker in the kitchen, so quickly switched on the back ring to full, filled a saucepan of water and placed it on the ring to boil. Anyone who interrupted her at her work would have a new face, melted on with boiling water. She then nipped through the neatly furnished lounge across the brown soft pile carpet to the front hall, pushing the latch down on the door lest anyone with a key should disturb her.

With her preparations complete, she made her way up the stairs to the bedrooms. This, usually, is where the booty lies. The two small bedrooms held nothing of interest for her. Now onto the master bedroom. She always liked to keep the best for last. Passing the double divan to her left and the white fitted wardrobes to her right, she headed for the white, four-high chest of drawers that held a red portable T.V. and two 'heaven-sent' jewellery boxes on top. Her pasty complexion elevated to pillarbox red in anticipation. She sat on the bed and opened them up to discover an Aladdin's cave of gold. Sovereign rings, chunky gold bracelets, three watches, ten gold chains, a solitary twenty-four carat gold sovereign coin, pendants and earrings. It was a jeweller's shop in a box.

'Yi haa!' she screamed inside, then closed her eyes and shook her head as though to make sure it wasn't a mirage. Her January, dull face lit up like the 4th of July and for a moment, just a moment she was transported from out of her mental burrow and far away from her festering abyss of an existence in a Woodend hovel flat with violent P, who beat her up more often than he didn't. Away from the ever present exposure to alcohol and depravation, where she was a grain of sugar in an ants nest of violence. Away from the mundane groove that her life had become. A deep smile creased her face and she pocketed the gold in a little black velvet, swag bag, her hands shook so much that she thought she might drop it. She hurried down the stairs and out of the house, leaving the lock still on the front door, but turning off the electric cooker on her exit, she was away, and it was only one-fifteen p.m. in the afternoon.

In her wake she left her second, and by far her greatest, error. It was my house she had just robbed.

Sharon with her big eyes and pretty, inviting smile capped by short jelled, dark hair that was sprightly and neat, approached our house. The three p.m. bus from town dropped her right outside. Her slight, curved frame, wasp waist and lady walk belied the ferocious fighting ability that her black belt stood evidence of, though you'd never have believed it by her affable nature and elfin-like gait.

When her key wouldn't turn in the lock she was baffled, but nothing more. 'Perhaps Geoff's in the garage and has locked the door for extra safety,' she thought as she wandered around the back. The kitchen door window was broken and the door ajar. Then she knew, but still tried to deny it to herself. 'Geoff's probably broken it by accident,' she told herself. When she finally got to the bedroom to find a lifetime's worth of jewellery gone, there was no denying the obvious. We'd been robbed! She sat on the bed not knowing what to do. Jewellery boxes upturned all over the bed. A paroxysm of tears built up and tried to explode in her eyes, but she held them back. That wasn't her way, though she did feel shocked beyond measure. We'd only been in the house six weeks, nobody gets robbed after only six weeks, do they? She'd been so happy, overflowing with the stuff, now this, some bastard, some dirty bastard had been in her house, her bedroom and rifled through her belongings.

She was veiled with an absolute feeling of helplessness. Her smarting eyes let out a single tear, she wished Geoff was home. He'd know what to do.

My golden Sierra Ghia purred and shuddered to a halt outside my house. My heart rate increased at the sight of a police car occupying my parking space. I knew something was wrong, I just hoped it was nothing too serious. I racked my brain: when was the last time I gave some one a dig? Have they reported me? Nothing came to mind, it had been weeks since I'd hit anyone and I was sure I'd taken that library book back. I made my way hastily into the house. There was muffled talking in the kitchen. As I entered the lounge from the main door so did Sharon from the kitchen.

"We've been burgled," was all she could muster. A feeling of great sadness ran through my body as I took her in my arms.

"Don't worry, I'll sort it out," I told her as I sympathetically rubbed her back. She feigned a smile. I returned one equally as false. My mind raced into overdrive, a thousand questions jamming the switchboard of my grey matter. The one most elevated and obvious being,

"Where the fuck do I start?" I went into the kitchen. Sharon's dad, a heavy set, handsome man in his fifties was on his knees tacking a piece of hardboard over the broken window (and why not, he does it so much better than I). A cocktail of feelings suffused my body, hate, sadness, revenge and confusion all failing to find a loading place in my mind, nor an exit from my body. I wanted to make it all alright, make Sharon smile again, give her an instant remedy.

"Ha, don't worry Shaz, it'll be Joe the burglar. When he realises it's our house he'll drop the goods back to us in a trice."

But I held no such remedies or revelations, only confusion and disdain. I felt helpless and hurt, so resorted to the obvious,

"Some bastard's gonna pay for this!"

A fresh faced policeman (aren't they all?), emerged from the hallway, sympathetic, kind and as helpless as us.

"Come down to the station love," he told Sharon, whose eyes were beginning to smart again. "When you feel a little better come and drop in a list of everything that's missing. Try not to touch anything until the fingerprints man has been."

I picked up my black, Wrawlings baseball bat from the brick fireplace, where it lay sentry for just such occasions (it's cheaper than a burglar alarm). I held it firmly by handle and head in left and right hand, tapping comfort into my swimming mind. My eyes glazed with hatred, the panda car pulled away from the outside of my house. Just this one act (the robbery, not the panda car nicking my space) seemed to wipe out the last six weeks of absolute bliss, of joyful bandanage, of plentiful hugs, laughs and smiles, of late night excited talks and early morning risings. Every evening for six weeks had been a juvenile Christmas Eve, every morning Christmas morning. The six weeks had been a plexus of jubilance, a harem of love, all decimated by the toxic pall of this fetid slag, who had robbed our house.

"Some bastard's gonna pay for this," I said again, to no one in particular.

"You can't just go around hitting people," (hey, let me be the judge of that) Sharon blurted out rather uncharacteristically, popping the cork of her self control.

"Don't fucking tell me what I can and can't do. As soon as I find out who's been in here I'm gonna fucking destroy them, and no cunt is going to stop me!" I shouted, even more uncharacteristically. This was the reverberative side of me that Sharon had never seen. I'd never even raised my voice to her before, nor her to me. We were, had been and hopefully always would be the proverbial love birds. She burst out of the room, and why not, my outburst was completely uncalled for.

"I think she's a little upset Geoff," interrupted the very observant Alan, Sharon's younger brother. I nodded a nod that was both apologetic and agreeing. They say you always hurt the ones you love. I quickly followed her up the stairs and gave her an apologising hug. We were both fraught and anxious and yes, helpless. The cold flame of hatred in my heart was eating my insides away like a corrosive. My thought infested forehead throbbed like a hammered thumb nail. Where to go, who to see, what to say, how to say it? I might hold the biography of a veteran fighter, but when it came to the skullduggery of the pilfering kind, I was a relative neophyte. What I did have though was determination and against people of this ilk I could be a master of intimidation, with justification as my ally. There were no lengths that I wouldn't go to, no methods or devices, fair or foul that I would not employ. I am a very affable chap, but on the flip side, when riled, can be a supercilious bastard, omnipotent to boot.

I hugged Sharon and felt her sadness (it felt sort of sad), picked up my bat and left my surreptitious abode on the start of my 'hunt for gold'.

The bat was to be a visual, people tend to listen to you more when you wield such an implement, also, when this saga was all over the presence of the former would be remembered a lot longer than my face or presence, (not that I intended to give any presents) just a forethought, a psychological implement, rather that a battering ram. I wanted people to say,

"He's a nutcase. He was running around with a huge bat. Don't fuck with this man. Give his property an extremely wide and respectful berth."

From my experience it always worked. Even the most pachyderm amongst the criminal fraternity would not court such madness, and besides all that, it was easier to hurt people with a bat than without one.

I knocked the door of the terraced, pre-war house that seemed acutely narrow. Dave, a tall, blond man in his late thirties answered, his eyes hit my bat, then shock hit his face. He was a friend who was in the know. He invited me into the front room, which was unclean though quite homely, his face, which looked as though it was made of Hong Kong plastic like a character out of Thunderbirds, froze in an uncomfortable smile. I told him my tale of woe and asked for names. I wanted to know who the local thieves were and who they dealt with, he'd lived here a long while and knew the local villains. Every area had one or two receivers, people who bought goods that were a little warm.

Longford's dealer, he informed me, was a man they called Duke. The name hinted at ominousness, but I didn't give a fuck. I wore my anger and ill-intent like a thorny crown. I handed my Karate business card, listing my qualifications in the world of combat and my phone number, to Dave;

"Tell anyone and everyone that I'm hunting for the person who stole my gold, and when I find them, I'm going to break their fucking legs." I lifted my bat to emphasise the seriousness of my intention. His pale complexion and frozen Thunderbirds smile told me that he believed me.

The truculent 'Hyde' in me vied with my usually diffident 'Jekyll' nature and was winning. I was seething with anger: not only had my possessions gone but my pride was severely dented. I'm ashamed to say that I thought I was above being robbed.

'No-one dare fuck with me, don't they know who I am? What I'll do to them?' I thought myself Longfond's omniscient God.

I'd made the fatal mistake of letting over-confidence creep into my mind and find a resting place therein. I hated myself for daring to feel superior, a trait I'd disliked in so many other people.

Smoothly I drove over the narrow Black Horse Road bridge and down along the tree-lined Black Horse Road in my gold Sierra, taking a shady left into the road that housed the 'Duke'.

The first door I knocked was the wrong door, but the friendly recipient, whose eyes disappeared amidst a thousand wrinkles, pointed me in the right direction, despite the presence of my 'Equaliser', the baseball bat.

"You're not going to hit him are you? He's my friend."

"No, no," I replied, "we're just gonna have a game of baseball." What did he think I was going to do with it, pick my nose? I wondered what kind of friend it was that sent a baseball bat wielding nutcase to a said 'friend's' door? He was either slavish to stupidity or a disgruntled neighbour aliasing as a friend.

Another door was knocked and another marble stare hit the bat I held so ominously. I told him my business and apologised for my unsolicited call. My invite into his warm, clean, modestly furnished front room, stretched not to my bat, so I left it at the front door of this terraced, pre-war house down a quiet cul-de-sac. I didn't need it really. My much practised, often used right hook seconded nicely if need be. His blonde, tall, attractive lady friend kindly offered me a cup of tea. I politely refused. The 'Duke' eyed me with suspicion. (I wouldn't have even let me in.) He was middle-aged with a crime weathered face capped by light receding hair. He looked 'John Wayne rugged' and earned, I guess, the tab 'Duke'. He tried to give me a hard look, and his effort wasn't bad, but I'd seen hard, and this wasn't it, though the mask would fool most. Again, I told my tale and proffered my business card and 'I'm gonna break legs' warning that was to become the epistle of this saga. He looked at my business card for a few seconds, he pondered on it, then his eyes lit up and he pointed to me, dropping the hard mask that hadn't fooled me anyway.

"Ah, you're Geoff Thompson." I admired his perception. "Wasn't it you," he continued, "that had your cheque stolen last year and hunted it down?" (Story in 'Watch my Back'.)

I smiled. I was flattered that my escapade had reached the ears of people who I knew not.

"Yea, that's right. That was a long time ago."

"You're not having much luck, are you?"

I shook my head. We talked a little more and he gave me another contact and his assurance that should my gold fall on his doorstep he'd redirect it back to me.

The contact he gave me was F, the second-hand dealer. F was a friend of mine from the stolen cheque saga so was on my list anyway. On the way to F's lay The Saracen's Head, The Coach and Horses, The Billiard Hall, The Griffen and Carneys, all Longford drinking holes. Within half an hour I'd visited all, left my card, my tale of woe and intentions to landlords/ladies and punters. My purpose here was twofold. I was not so naive as to believe that they'd ring me up if they'd heard tell of my estranged loot, though even an off-chance was worth a shot. Rather I wanted everyone in the district to know that my house had been robbed. I wanted it to be a common talking point in the locals so that eventually the news of my hunt would fall on the ears of the guilty party and that I wasn't a man to take it lying down. It wasn't just my gold at stake, nor even just my pride, the security of my new house was in question. It was important to me that every crook around knew what to expect if they fucked with me. There was no burglar alarm better than that of fear (or a belt round the face with a bat) and if I had to emulate someone to get the point across, then so be it. Most of these thieves were languid bastards anyway, so it wouldn't take a lot of doing.

When I arrived at F the dealer's abode, news of my hunt had already reached him, in fact. When I entered the cosy front room of his terraced, Longford Road house, the 'Duke' was sat there with a cup of tea. Gosh the room was nice. The last time I came here was a year before, hunting for a cheque that had been stolen from me. Then the room seemed plain, and though clean, in need of a face-lift. Now it sported an expensive, immaculate leather Chesterfield suite, sat neatly on deep piled axminster and a fireplace built from hand-made brick that chimneyed to the ceiling. Fate had obviously blown some nice gear into his second-hand business. F smiled, showing a missing front tooth, his dark skin creased his face, his long, Apache, black hair lay shining and flat, cascading down to his shoulders. F ran a local second hand shop and was a real character who knew everyone and everything about local crime. As I entered the front room the 'Duke' rose and greeted me like an old friend. I sensed by his darting look to my right side that he liked me all the better without my bat. D, F's attractive, blonde wife smiled shyly up from the Chesterfield. I sensed she liked me and was at home with people of my ilk, her brother and late father had been of a similar gait.

After the usual pleasantries we got down to business: who'd been in my house? F dealt with all the thieves and if he didn't know, no-one would.

"How did they gain entry to the house?" F asked. I wondered what difference it made. Apparently, it made a lot.

"Through the back door."

"How?" Another stupid question, I thought, but he's the boss.

"By smashing the window," I replied, veiling my bafflement.

"And what was taken?"

"Gold."

"Nothing else. Just gold?"

"Yea, I've got loads of stuff in the house as well, but nothing else was touched."

F looked across at D knowingly, asking with his eyes her permission to 'tell'. She half smiled, giving it to him. People like F and D would usually die before informing on anyone. Let you pull out their toenails first, but this was different. I wasn't police; I was one of them.

"Sounds like M," he said with an ever-so-slight hint of reluctance and a little whistle as the words left his front-toothless mouth. "She breaks glass and takes gold. There's a couple at it, but this is her gaff. I'd be very surprised if it's not her. She used to slaughter all her gear to me, but we had words about a year ago, and she deals somewhere else now." He thought for a moment, then looked at D.

"You know her D, dark haired bird, with the big severe mouth." He shot his glance to me.

"Horrible piece she is, evil mouth on it. Just got married to Scotch P from Woodend." D nodded her agreement.

"Right dirty slag," she concluded, descriptively.

So, I was looking for a 'right dirty slag called M with an evil mouth on it'. Well, that'd narrow it down a bit.

When the conversation reached an impasse, I thanked them cordially for their help and left with the name inscribed on my brain, and a piece of cigarette paper with my next contact on. I stood outside the house of 'Fency', so called because he fenced anything from cheap ladies underwear to Armani suits, from job lots of kids sweets to hard drugs. If crime pays, his cheque must have still been in the post because the street in Foleshill that held his house looked like a bomb site in Beirut. It never ceased to amaze me that these so called crooks and drug dealers who purported to earn 'good money' lived nearly always in the pits of deprivation. Either the 'good money' was squandered or it simply wasn't 'good money'. People are always saying,

"Hey, John earns some coin on those drugs." Oh really, is that why he's still living in a shithole in Woodend? 'Fuck off!'. Some of them do earn good money, I know, but probably only one per cent have the intelligence to do anything other than squander it.

I knocked the paint-flaking door. The four square, glass windows it held were filmed with dirt. As the door opened the smell of take-away food, dogs and dodgy central heating hit me like a warm breeze. A churlish, marble stare challenged me. 'Fency', unlike 'Duke', needed not a mask for unwelcome strangers. He was hard, shorter than myself at five foot ten inches, with mousey, light hair and a battle scar embedded like a moon river across the right side of his nose. He chewed his dinner and stared up at me, his teeth were the colour of banana skin and his face held a grimace even as he chewed.

"Yea?" he said, without interrupting his chewing. He was obviously a man of few words.

"F the dealer sent me," I said, not really sure where to start. He looked behind me, then to my left and right. Was this a set-up? Was I a copper? Who the fuck was I?

"You'd better come in."

If I thought the street was scruffy then I was in for a surprise when I saw his front room: it held a scattering of what looked like the debris from an explosion in a dustbin. Old chip papers, crisp packets empty and half-so, magazines, newspapers all looked at home and in place on the floor and littered on and around the furniture. An old tinfoil Chinese take-away tray lay forlorn under the television, with its sauce-stained base dry and hard from age. (Poor bastard, we've got a video under our telly.) This was a scruffy front room. Everyone has the right to be dirty, but this man was abusing the privilege. To match the war-torn living space, I expected his woman to be a virago, Amazon-type girl with child bearing hips, a Henry

Cooper left hook, callused knuckles and a piano keyboard smile. I was surprised to be confronted by a coffee-proffering blonde, slight lady with a sweet voice and disposition. I declined the kind offer of coffee; I'm sure it would have taken her ages to sandblast a cup clean for me.

I introduced myself and told of my business, but 'Fency' still seemed a little unapproachable. Understandable I guess, as I was a stranger asking unsolicited questions.

His eyes seemed in a permanent state of squint, and he was still chewing, yet there didn't seem to be any food in his mouth.

"You came highly recommended," I said, trying to sweeten him up a little, and loosen his tongue (that's probably what he was chewing). This seemed to placate, a little, his over-active suspicious mind, and over the next fifteen minutes he spilled all his contacts, dealings and general theories on the histrionics of crime and its workings. The name M was mentioned again.

Eventually I managed to get out of the house without catching anything (no easy feat I can tell you). Another handshake saw me back on the road, head still pounding, my violent alter ego dying to burst forth and teach someone a lesson. I'd got a name, so it was a start.

Many, many more houses and public houses were visited, tomorrow I'd visit all of the second-hand shops.

"You'll never find out who's done it Geoff," said my friend smartly as we stood talking on the Devon door.

"I fucking will," I snapped back. (I was a little tense.)

"D'ya reckon?" he asked, disbelievingly.

"I don't reckon, I know. I might not get my gold back, but I'm gonna dish out some pain when I find out who's had it." His mouth curved into a disdainful smirk. He didn't think so.

Another fucking sleepless night, tossing and turning. We, Sharon and I had to sleep on a mattress on the floor of the spare room, less we disturb vital evidence in our own room.

"Try not to touch anything until the fingerprints man has been," we were told by the ever-so-sympathetic copper who'd seen and done it all before. Nothing in life was about to shock this man. Burglaries were way down at the bottom of his shopping list of stress/shock related incidents. He'd once had to bag up the cadaver of an unfortunate, born-again Christian whose skull was split wide and gaping, issuing blood and brain everywhere and whose lung lay precariously on his chest where the home made killing implement, that looked something a kin to a sickle, had left it on its retraction from his convulsing body. The bestower, a devil worshipping, brain dead, had taken offence at his preaching. No. Burglaries were definitely mundane by comparison.

Again, I was in the company of stress related insomnia. Sharon was there too. All night I could feel her sleepless sadness. It was almost tangible. I pulled her close to me and kissed her gently on the lips, hoping to assuage her pain, knowing nothing could. The damage was done, though I've got to say, she did bare the sadness stoically. As our eyes held a helpless grip, we accepted tactically that stress would be our constant companion until this thing was resolved.

You don't realise how many second-hand shops there are in one city until you've cause to visit them. There are fucking loads. The next morning I made it my business to visit them all in the hope that I could block off all the lines of exit that my gold might take. I knew it would be offered around one of these places, so I had to let them (the shop owners) know that if they bought it, I'd be after them too. I wasn't rude, nor impolite, I just planted the seed of retribution in their brains. It worked because one of my friends in the second hand trade said that all the dealers were ringing each other up:

"Who's this mad bastard, Geoff Thompson? Have you had his gear?"

"No."

"Well don't take it. He's a fucking nutcase," etc.

I didn't need to tell the dealers that I was going to break their legs, the implication would be enough.

"You tell them," I'd say, wagging a condemning finger, "that I'm on their trail, and when I find them, which I will, I'm gonna break their fucking legs."

The added expletive helped to enforce my resolve. If you want to get through to people of the criminal ilk you have to be able to talk the talk, if and when necessary, walk the walk.

The man in front of me, over twenty stone and as cool as winter snow, was, in this city, 'the man'. His head looked like a pea on a mountain, his body was big enough to warrant grid references, he was the biggest thing I'd ever seen without an engine and he spoke with an authoritative and confident voice, (as you do when you're twenty-two stone). 'A' was also my close friend. On hearing of my loss he made a few discreet enquiries. When I visited him at his abode I was pleased to hear the name M for the third time, but it wasn't until I visited the pub that I had absolute confirmation.

"Whoever it is that's had my gold," I told the heavy set landlord, "cut their arm on my glass door as they went in."

His eyes lit up and he ushered me across to one side. He lifted thumb and forefinger to chin and thought deeply before speaking, the comfortable pouch that hung above his belt expanded to almost bursting point as he sighed: I thought it might push me out of the room. He had to be careful about what he said, he didn't want to be thought of as a grass, comebacks from the people in question could be heavy if they knew it was he who told.

"There was a girl in here yesterday at about one-thirty p.m. with a cut on her arm."

I suppressed my delight.

"Was her name M by any chance?" I asked, almost bursting with glee.

"Yea, that's right. Married to Scotch P."

YI AHH! I'd got her. I'd fucking got her.

"Be careful though, Geoff," he continued. "P's a nasty piece of work, good with a blade."

"We'll see," I said, as my heart raced with a cocktail of fear, excitement and exhilaration.

I opened my front door and walked deftly across the brown carpeted front hall to the living room. Sharon was busy ironing.

"I've got her, I've fucking got her," I told her excitedly, then regaled her with the hows and wherefores. Sharon was equally excited: we shared a hug, her supple body fitted mine like a glove. We both felt elated because we knew that this thing was nearly over, all I had to do now was set the scene.

"I want to come with you when you get her," Sharon said.

"No! Thanks, but no. I'll do it. I know you want to go and I admire your bottle, but I have to do it on my own." She did have the bottle but, I don't know, I just didn't feel it was right for her to come with me.

Anyway, now I had a definite name, I was on my way. A quick coffee and I was off again, this time with the cold flame of hatred blazing in my heart. Bell Green club, Bell Inn, Rose and Crown, Green Man, Golden Fleece and one or two more pubs were visited in the next hour. This time though, I was hunting for a specific prey, Scotch P. I knew he drank in all of these places, specifically the club. I would confront him and demand what was mine. If he so much as breathed erratically, I would destroy him on the spot.

If he wanted to 'go', he'd better be fucking good with that knife. Every pub that I entered that afternoon, I prepared myself to fight him and anyone with him. That's the only way that you can cope with these type of situations. Imagine the worst case scenario, then tell yourself that 'you can handle it'. Every pub that I entered that afternoon hadn't seen P today. I handed each pub a card and said,

"Tell P I'm looking for him."

I walked into the club, a typical working men's club with a large bar and a scattering of cheap tables and chairs. I approached the bar to be greeted by a young girl with more make-up than face, and more tits than dress. She had a kind smile (the kind that frit' the living day lights out of me), the girls that worked the bars in places like these were tougher than Samsonite luggage.

"I'm looking for Scotch P. Is he in?" I scanned the bar as I spoke.

"That's 'is family over there." She nodded her head at a rough group of people sat at the back of the bar room. As she nodded her make-up moved, making her 'two faced' and her boobs nearly fell out of her dress (I contemplated asking her another question, I felt one more nod might have seen a spillage).

I approached the table that sat about eight of the roughest looking specimens this side of the American deep south, a Scottish family from the Gourbels with more time served than a prison Governor, this family could 'rough' for Scotland. It took me a few seconds to fathom the men from the women (the women were the ones with the bigger muscles and deeper scars). They were all playing cards, none looked up as I approached, but that was the game, it's meant to imply that you're 'not a threat', in fact so little of a threat that we're not even going to look up from the table. I knew the game, I liked it, I'd played it many times before. I counter attacked this by drilling a stare into them one by one. In Coventry a stare is a subliminal 'challenge to fight'. My stare said just that, 'I'm ready to fight you all', my counter was acknowledged by a nod from one of the men. The nod looks like a friendly gesture, really it's a bottle drop.

My heart beat began to race.

"Where's P?" I asked, hiding the quaver in my voice.

His brother, long hair with a face like a collapsed lung, threw me the kind of cold look that was supposed to emblazon 'cool' but I knew it was veiling 'scared', if he wasn't scared we'd have been fighting already. The rest of the family carried on as though I wasn't there, feigning disconcern, though I knew that they were concerned and that the very act of me entering their lair (it wasn't quite so tidy as a lair) alone had unnerved them. It hinted of psychotic, I knew it would, that's exactly why I did it (maybe I'm a little psychotic as well?). As the great Sun Tzu said twenty five centuries ago (he never actually said it to me personally), 'If you know your enemy and know yourself, you need not fear the result of a hundred battles'. I did know my enemy, and I definitely knew myself, (I'd lived with me for over thirty years) Sun Tzu also said that the supreme act of war was to subdue the enemy without fighting. That was also big on my game plan. By the time I actually find the man a dozen of his friends and family would have already told him that I was looking for him, he'll have put the feelers out to see who I am and what kind of firepower I hold (if in fact he didn't know already) and the feedback will have scared him shitless, if my ploy worked that is, if not we'd be fighting and I was already well prepared for that.

"He's nort hearr!" came the thick Glaswegian reply. Casually, I skimmed my business card across the card table, and fixed his gaze until he turned away.

"Tell 'im Geoff Thompson's looking for 'im. He ought t' ring."

At that I smiled, turned and walked out of the club. As I did so I could feel the hairs (what few I have left) on the back of my neck rise in anticipation of a 'Judas' attack. It never came.

Wednesday, five p.m., I arrived back home from an afternoon's bricklaying, done mostly in auto-mode. My mind was far away from bricks and mortar, an eternity lost from spirit level and jointing iron, I was oblivious to the deep ache my lower back dispersed (that old yellow streak again). My mind was obsessed by and with revenge, turmoiled by violent thoughts and geared up totally to the recovery of my stolen gold. I was beginning to feel a little weak, stress of this intensity takes its toll and weakens you immeasurably, the fight isn't just in the pubs/clubs when you actually confront your antagonists, it's with yourself, every minute of the day, a continual battle between Mr Negative fighting Mr Positive with Mr Negative trying to drag you down into the ever decreasing spiral of depression and only the inspiring granite of Mr Positive keeping you above water.

Sharon's pretty face cheered me up, as it always did. Her big, bright, sea-green eyes sparkled a welcome that I'd come to love. I kissed her and took her in my arms holding her tightly and savoured the perfumed smell from her soft neck. I kissed her gently on the lips.

"You've had three calls from a Scottish chap," she said. "I told him you'd be back at five-thirty p.m."

I smiled.

"How did he sound?" I asked, looking for clues as to how he was handling it.

"He sounded a little worried," she smiled back.

"Good, that's exactly how I want him." Worried men are easier to mould into supplication.

I relaxed in the grey/pink suit and sipped my hot coffee. I usually really enjoy a relax and a drink, but not in times of stress. Nothing is enjoyed fully, even love making is relegated to a bland performance, at best, lacklustre (that's my excuse anyway). I hate, and hated stress, but expected its company at such times as this and nei-

ther accepted nor rejected the feeling, just lived with it.
To try and reject it only causes more inner turmoil, just
ignore it like you would perhaps a poll tax bill, and eventually it will slide away, having no ledge upon which to
hook. The tring of the telephone broke my daydream and
made me jump. Sharon came from out of the kitchen to
spectate. I slowly ambled over to the sonorous, white
phone, but didn't pick it up straight away. Let him sweat:
the extra few rings will kill him.

"Hello," I said, eventually lifting the receiver, my stomach
clenching in apprehension, an almost audible shake in
my voice.

"Geoff," came the soft, Scottish, disembodied voice on
the other end of the line.

"This is P. I hear you've been looking for me." Without waiting for my answer he continued, "Somebody sayd
you think ma messus has rorbed yuar husse. A've had a
werrd wiy' 'er and she seys she knows nethin' aboot it."
I'd expected him to deny it initially, but it still disappointed me when he did, I'd hoped it would be easier.

"P, you know an' I know that she's 'ad my gold. So,
don't play games wi' me, y' know 'oo I am and what I'll
do. I'm trying to be nice about this so don't take the piss.
I'm a fair man and I'm givin' you one chance. Get m'
gold back and that'll be the end of it, if not, you're gonna'
'ave big problems. I don't wan' 'oo 'ave t' come t' your
'ouse."

"Ded you come to my husse las' neight?" He quiv-
ered.

"No, not las' night," I replied, suppressing a smile.
Someone obviously knocked his door the night before and
because he thought it was me he'd not answered it. I had
visions of him and M hiding behind the settee holding
the dog's mouth shut in case he barked and gave them
away.

"I'll give you a week to get it back," I concluded.

"O.K.," he said quietly. I put the phone down.

In that moment of negotiation, a week had seemed to me to be reasonable and a short time to wait. By Friday my head was shot to pieces with the thought of having to wait another five days, and I was beginning to regret giving him such a long time. I should have demanded it there and then. Everyday I waited I got more frustrated and angry, I wanted to go to his house and drag him and her out and demand what was mine. I wondered if I could realistically expect ever to see my gold again? Did he agree to get it back only in the hope that after a week or so I'd let it drop, or perhaps he'd find a sudden surge of bravery and defy me to get it back off him, perhaps using the seven days to gather an army? I decided to give him the week as I'd agreed, then if it was fruitless, I'd visit his house at four a.m. in the morning and pebble dash the house with him. I'd batter the pair of them in their bed. To give myself some time, I'd ring the Bell Green Police station with a red herring (I hear they like fish) on the other side of the district to give me 'in and out' time.

His second floor flat lay on the edge of the roughest part of Woodend, in 'P' Close, recently the area of mass battles with the police. There were more broken noses here than at a boxers' convention, and anyone that couldn't fit five expletives into one sentence was classed as a wimp. I watched the news the night before, it said 'twenty dead in Sarajevo' . . . that's just a stag night in Wood End. His flat backed onto a field and an industrial estate that lay deserted by night. I parked my car on the narrow road at the beginning of the estate, just a couple of hundred yards from the flats. I tucked my Samurai sword under my long coat and walked slowly down the grass hill and across a little field to 'P' Close. The moonless, early evening sky relegated me, gratefully, to a shadow. The smell of burning rubbish in the distance wafted into my lungs. Even the dark of night, though, didn't hide the graffiti-seared ribaldry of these Woodend hovels, two high and long buildings, akin to army barracks.

Burnt out cars lay abandoned on the edge of the estate, the kids played in them by day and dreamed of becoming racing drivers (most end up becoming 'joy riders'). Dull lights emitted from the yellow, cigarette stained nylon net curtains that stuck to the condensation-soaked windows, the ones that weren't boarded up, inspiring apathy and deep gut feelings of loneliness. I recalled many, many years before when the council offered me and my first, new wife, one of these Woodend flats, thinking we would desperately snatch it up. The proffered flat was boarded up and smelt like a tramp's sock. It was in such a bad state of repair that I was sure they'd sent me to the wrong address. When it appeared they hadn't, I told them,

"If ya spend five grand on cleaning it up, I might pura horse in it."

Many of the people occupying these kennels though, were in worse repair themselves than the flats, so I guess it worked well. Between the blocks of flats was an absolute concrete maze of walls and paths and entryways. It looked as though it was designed by a mugger. None of the numbers seemed to follow (handy if you've got the police looking for you). As I searched for the appropriate number, my longing was to be away from this dull, gaunt street, the sad feelings of pity in my stomach burgeoned the longer I stayed. But it was important that I targeted P's flat, so that (if and when) I could be in and out quickly when the dirty deed was done. My eye caught the glow of one of the few lamp lights that wasn't smashed and it brought to mind a London street in the Twenties. It was as though, on walking into this street, I'd gone back in time seventy years. I felt privileged that I didn't have to live here. Its depravation left an acidic taste in my mouth, I wondered if the council officials dishing out these slums had ever seen the state of them. I doubted it. It was said that there were so many burglaries in this area that you daren't close the window at night for fear of trapping someone's fingers.

When I finally did find my number it took all my will-power not to go, there and then, and knock the door, demand my gold, beat the pair of them to a pulp and be away. No! I disciplined myself. I'd made a deal and that was it, no door knocking until the week was up. I also knew that my temper was volcanoing to a ten on the Richter scale and knocking his door might just shoot it off the page completely. Then I'd be looking at a charge of aggravated burglary carrying a possible seven years in prison: the courts don't look kindly on vigilantes. I could actually go to prison for retrieving my own gold from a thief. Great, isn't it?

Reluctantly, I jogged back to my car, timing myself. Thirty seconds. Probably two minutes to get in his flat, do the job and out, thirty seconds back to the car, and another minute for miscellaneous. That's four minutes in all. I wondered if P and M knew just how close the mantle of retribution and revenge lay. I drove away from the pedantic Woodend satisfied in the knowledge that I had set the scene, just in case.

I'd been intending to insure the contents of the house ever since I moved in, but never actually got around to it, as is always the way. A quick phone call to 'Sheffield' Johnny sorted that little problem, a bit of post-dated insurance was assured. June, he told me, worked for an insurance company and was crazy about him, she'd sort it out.

John was a very charismatic man with a thirst for crime and a hunger for violence. He was also hugely funny with an uncannily accurate philosophy on life. He sported long silver white hair and a beard to match. A heavy scar, picked up in a bar in Glasgow (he only went in for a laugh, he came out in stitches) split the right side of the beard neatly in two. He wore the scar proudly: to people like

John the scar gave him character, it was a badge of battle. His whole body was a canvas of Indian ink Tattoo, and he was forever telling young ladies 'what nice tits' they had, and being dumbfounded when they were offended. He couldn't understand it, he thought he was giving them a compliment.

"Get yer sen a dorg," he told me in that deep, Scottish accent. "Bearter than any alarm, an' all 'is bull-shit aboot having to take them for a walk everyday, don't listen to it son. I've had dorgs for twenty years and never took them for a walk yet."

The police finger prints man knocked my front door, it was late afternoon, almost the end of the working day. Ours was just one of a myriad of houses he'd been to that week, ten that day. I invited him in. He was a weather beaten, handsome type of man, in an ill-fitting grey suit, equally grey white shirt with top button unfastened and tie loosened in a kind of 'bedraggled' look. His 'trod on' leather black shoes looked like they'd done a dozen marathons. His thin pale lips (they matched his attire) appeared frozen in a look of disdain displaying that 'pissed off' type of look (like most policemen I'd come into contact with) that only came from years and years of chasing criminals that you knew you were not going to catch, not because they were master criminals, nor because you were not good at your job, but because of 'the system', a system that seemed more in favour of the 'law breaker' than the 'law abider'. He'd recently had to charge a man with assault for battering a burglar he'd caught 'in the act' in his own house (he shouldn't have done that, it's against the law). How do you tell someone that you agree with what they've done but . . . you've got to arrest them anyway.

The irony of the whole job of policing is that, even before they visit a burgled house they've got a pretty good idea who's done the job, but they can't arrest them with out absolute evidence. The way the law stands they've practically got to catch the criminals in the act AND get a full confession.

In the Nineties the job of the policeman is like playing a game of football against a team with movable goal posts, a blind referee and a team captain that's not on your side.

Coffee and biscuits were proffered, he eagerly accepted. The poor man looked, by his wan face, like he hadn't eaten in ages. The trouble was, people who've been robbed never seem to be in the mood to offer refreshments, mostly they are crest fallen and untalkative, the last thing you want to do is ask someone who has just had their life's belongings stolen for coffee and biscuits. He only ever did it once out of desperation when he felt in grave danger of emaciation, the cold look he received in way of reply frightened him for life of ever asking again.

"Look," he told us straight, through a biscuit filled mouth, "the chances of ever seeing your gold again, or in fact of catching the people responsible for taking it, are negligible. You've got more chance of winning the pools. I've visited forty houses this week and believe me, you've been lucky [Oh yea! really lucky], some of the victims have had the whole house emptied, everything they owned gone in one go. Some of them are old people who have not only lost their belongings they've also lost their will to live. Some of them never recover from the trauma that these bastards cause. You're both young and strong, you'll get over it. They probably never will."

All this statement did was harden my resolve to 'do it myself'. If our kind friend the finger prints man, (who by the way, paid a little too much attention to Sharon for my liking, thank you very much), thought he was getting a second cup of coffee and biscuits for nothing, he was badly mistaken. No, we subjected him to a half hour's talk

through our holiday snaps. That'll teach him to accept a
second cup.

To say I was pissed off with waiting was an understatement. By Monday I was as agitated as an aspen in
the wind, so I decided to pay my friend a visit. The Rose
and Crown lay, daringly, just off the Bell Green Road,
one level high, with lounge and bar entrances to left and
right respectively. Not an unattractive pub as pubs go,
though sparse inside with a scattering of tables and chairs
and a run of soft seating by the bayed bar window that
sat the old, drunk and infirm. To the right of the entrance
sat six, all uniform in their hard and scarred faces. They
looked like they were waiting to enter an 'ugly' contest.

In my bright red and green Nike tracksuit, Fila boots
and leather Fila cap, I strolled in, my confident gait hiding my churning stomach, the result of my much over-
worked adrenal gland. Straight to the bar, the barman's
eyes darted from me to the unruly group in the corner.

"That them?" I said evenly without turning my head
to look. He nodded. There were a few other people sat
around the bar who watched with interest as I approached
the table. I was expecting the worst, a fight. In any situation such as this, I always prepared myself for the absolute worst thing that could happen and then got my mind
into the appropriate gear. Anything less than the worst
was a prize. Up until now I had never met P and had
only had vague descriptions given to me (wanker,
arsehole etc.) so on arriving at the table I didn't know
which was he (they all looked like wankers and arseholes
to me). Nobody looked up, hoping maybe that I might
just disappear. The landlord looked over from the bar anx-
iously, he didn't want trouble in his pub. There was an
audible tension in the air.

I approached the Adams family.

To my right a heavy set man in his early twenties with
a face like a burglar's bulldog and a neck twitch to match
Tyson's, he had a bulbous nose that had 'target' written

all over it, next to him P's brother that I'd already met in the club, looking down at the table to avert my glare, then a man with a long E.T. neck and a tight small face, mostly hidden by his over sized baseball cap, the horrendous scar that ran down his right cheek was as wide as the blade that put it there, and as ugly as a troll's woman, an older man next to him with dark cropped hair and an involuntary smile and darting eyes that wanted to meet mine but dare not.

The air was thick with smoke and tension as I looked down at them wearing my hardest face and employing a walk that said to any one who knew 'walks' 'I don't give a fuck'.

I stopped at the table, opened my eyes wide and grimaced my mouth, the adrenaline was rushing around my body like a crazed fly trapped in a jam jar. I used the Duck syndrome to hide my fear, calm above the waters, legs going like fuck underneath. I was here now, and I was ready to do it. They were all sitting down so I had a temporary edge, I stood slightly back from the table so that I could kick the head off the first and closest to me if any of them gave me grief, then I'd get into the rest before they had a chance to react. Hopefully the first two or three would be out of the game before the others knew what was happening. I remembered the words of the legendary Japanese sword master Musashi, 'when dealing with multiple opponents you must attack first and keep attacking until the danger subdues'. Yep. That sounded good to me.

My ploy was to ask for P by name; if the reply was hostile in any way, shape or form I'd go in to 'psycho mode' and attack everything that moved, straight away. I didn't expect to win against six opponents, but I felt sure that I could remove a nose and a couple of ears before they could get on top of me. I'd definitely leave my mark. Do I sound brave? I didn't feel brave, I was shitting myself. This may sound barbaric, but that's what you need when you're dealing with 'Barbarians', after all you can't be a pussycat if you're fighting a tiger, also, somebody that you've 'marked' serves as a lifetime's walking billboard advertising 'YOU' as a man 'not to fuck with'.

None fixed my gaze. Yes, I liked this, this was a good sign.

"P," I said, with a hint of authoritative malice in my voice. I was shocked at their response: I was expecting some kind of animosity, but got none. Instead, they universally pointed to P. Even his brother sat there pointing a condemning finger, (kill him not me!) - so much for family loyalty. P's head shot around to catch a glimpse of me, our eyes met, mine hard and determinedly glaring, his swathed in supplication. A deep scar underlined his cheek bone, a scruffy uncut beard covered most of his whey face, all topped by the customary canvas baseball cap sported by most of Coventry's criminal youth. Bits of his light, thin hair pushed out sparingly from the sides of the hat like a scarecrow (no disrespect to scarecrows), he may have looked like a scarecrow but he wasn't doing much scaring at the moment. His shoulders and back hunched forward like a frightened cat and I had the urge to kick him clean out of the chair, but I resisted (I'm good like that).

"OUTSIDE!" I ordered. He jumped out of the chair and followed me without demur. Outside I lined him up as a matter of course. The busy Bell Green traffic hummed in the background, shoppers walked past oblivious to what was occurring, someone getting a 'dig' in this district was no more unusual that someone getting a parking ticket in London centre.

P fidgeted involuntarily and kept his hands in his blue, stained tracksuit, pockets emblazoning supplication. This was subliminally telling me that he didn't want to fight. I

let my hands hang loosely by my sides, this told him that
I was ready to fight. I stared at his weasel face and wondered whether I shouldn't destroy him where he stood.
Crush him flatter than a shadow. His chin looked tempt-
ingly close and mighty suspect. It would be easy, I knew,
to dish out a little pain here just to satisfy my flagging
ego, but I couldn't do it. I'd given my word that if he
delivered the goods, that would be the end of it. My word
meant a lot to me. I also felt a little sorry for him, though
I shouldn't have. He'd stabbed many before me and lived
a life of violence. Violence was his way: the fact that he
looked scared meant nothing. A frightened man if pushed
too far is a very dangerous man capable of very dangerous acts. The key to keeping someone frightened is to
make them feel that there is a way out, give them a little
hope. If they feel that there is no hope then they become
desperate, employing desperate measures. Many a good
man has been defeated chasing a 'beaten' man. Some of
my friends had said,

"Give it 'im anyway," but I couldn't go back on my
word. Even in this volatile environment you are only as
good as your word. There may be other situations in the
future where my word may be my saving grace, if it was
broken now it could be my 'coup de grace'.

I checked the pub door to make sure that his companions hadn't followed. They hadn't, we were alone.

"Where's my gear, man?" I attacked.

"I've got it, Geoff, I've got it," he spluttered, his voice
guttural Glaswegian. He must have felt sure that he was
about to get a dig.

"I've rung you three times today already. I'll bring it
to the club tonight."

I eyed him suspiciously. Had he really got it, or was
he just trying to save himself a hiding and buy a little
time?

"You've definitely got it?" I asked.

"Yea, yea. I'll bring it to the club tonight, seven-thirty p.m."

"Don't let me down, P," I said evenly, hiding my inner elation. Then as an after thought, "No, don't meet me at the club, you know where your flat is?" He nodded hesitantly, of course he knew where it was. "Meet me on the field at the back of your block of flats." His eyes shot forward like a cartoon cat trapped by the neck in a window. My ploy had the desired effect, his mouth fell open like a cash register and he blurted out,

"I knew you'd find out where I lived, I knew it."

I knew he'd react like that when I told him I knew where he lived.

"And another thing, P, tell M that my street is out of bounds from now on, tell her to keep away."

"I will," he conceded, and then, "I gave her a slap for ye, Geoff, t' teach her a lesson." This was his way of buying my favour. He didn't realise that it wasn't for sale.

"Good," I said, and I meant it. P's theory on handling women is that they are a little like gardens: every now and then they need a good dig.

At this I left, happy in the knowledge that I was nearly there, though I was still not sure I could believe him. I hoped, for his sake, that he wasn't lying. If he was lying I'd have to re-emburse myself out of his face (by the look of his face someone had already beaten me to it).

My plan now was to meet P that evening on the green at the back of his flat in 'P' Close, get out of my car as he approached, with my four foot long Samurai sword (just to cabbage him). I wouldn't hit him nor even threaten him with it, I'd stick it in the grass next to my feet (being very careful not to snip my toes). Just the presence of it would be enough to frighten him shitless, and then spread a 'Geoff Thompson's fucking crazy' rumour around Woodend like a dose in a brothel. Propaganda was a great psychological weapon in World War II, so why not, I thought, use a little of it myself?

P obviously thought my reasons for the secluded meeting were so that I could retrieve my gold and give him a thorough thraping, just as I knew his idea of meeting at the much populated club was to ensure, because of the presence of witnesses, that I didn't give him the said thraping. After all, just by the nature of it, pain was uncomfortable and best avoided. He'd had a bit of it in his time judging by his battle scarred 'boat race' and wasn't about to court any more, thank you very much. What P didn't realise was, I was a man of my word, a gentleman, a rarity in violent twentieth century Coventry. Another thing he obviously didn't realise was that if I did want to 'cane' him, a few witnesses wouldn't stop me from doing so. I'm stupid like that, if I decide to hit someone, I don't care if the Lord Mayor or Chief of Police is watching, they're gonna have it.

At the thought of the aforementioned 'pain', he got his sister to ring me up at five p.m. and say that he'd been arrested and she would come in place of him with my gold. A cop out, I know, but who gives a fuck, as long as I get back what's mine, I'm not bothered who hands it over.

Seven-fifteen p.m., Sharon kissed me goodbye, the worried look in her eyes belied her stoical front (and what a nice front it was too). She handed me my sword, bat and steel fist, see what a good girl she is, I could have easily forgot them. I felt a little like a factory worker going to do a shift, instead of my lady handing me a flask and sandwiches she hands me my killing implements. I probably wouldn't use them but I'd take them just in case it was a set-up and I arrived to find a team waiting in the shadows of Bell Green for me. Goodness knows, I'd made enough enemies there over the years. My friend Alan had advised against the sword, because, as he said,

"If there is a team there waiting for you, you'll use it and half of Bell Green will be walking around with bits missing."

The thing is, though, if they do set me up, it's what they deserve anyway. Al had also offered to go with me as had John 'Awesome' Anderson and many others, but the way I saw it, it had to be done on my own, anyway, it adds to the aftermath of propaganda if you're brave, crazy or stupid enough to 'deal' in Woodend on your lonesome.

I arrived at the club car park, which is also the car park for the Bell Green shopping centre, five minutes early. Big mistake! Five minutes may not seem long, but in times of stress, facing possible violence and with time distortion twisting a knife into your already clenching guts, it's a fucking eternity where every possible occurrence goes through your mind and your arsehole goes from the size of a sixpence to the size of a dustbin lid.

To the left of me was the back entrance to some of the shops in the precinct (these entrances are used more often by the punters than the front entrance). To my right, down about four steps, was the two level working men's club. Directly in front of me were the twelve foot high rear walls of some derelict communal garages that ran the entire length of the two hundred foot car park. Behind me was a long, high run of privet hedge, that looked precariously out of place in this concrete 'farm' they call Bell Green.

There was only one entrance to this 'mugger friendly' car park and two exits (the second being via ambulance). I'd entered the enemy's lair and wasn't my arse letting me know about it. Every car that entered the dark car park looked ominous, every group of people approaching, scarifying. I wanted to turn and run away to some warm sanctuary far from crazy and aggressive challenging eyes, hidden from a thousand scowling faces and ten thousand acidic voices. I wanted to be anywhere but here. These seconds before battle scared me most, weakened

me immeasurably, made me sad and lonely beyond com-
prehension. Everything inside me said, RUN, RUN, RUN,
and only the captaining granite of self-control held me
together. These seconds before battle are the hardest,
harder than the fighting, harder than the training. They're
just physical, quite easy by comparison. Adversity has
an uncanny way of putting your life into perspective, of
making you appreciate the finer things in life, like a walk
in the park, a cup of tea by the fire, lying in a warm bed
with a loving mate listening to an orchestra of rain playing a symphony on the window pane. All of the things
whose beauty had lain hidden behind the curtain of familiarity re-expose themselves and spring into life as you
see them being taken away from you. Then and only then
do you see and appreciate their true merit. I unashamedly prayed that I wasn't about to lose them to a cold
blade on an even colder evening. When this was over, by
fuck, was I going to enjoy those fine things.

All the time that these feelings burgeoned I kept a hard,
even look on my face as though nothing frightened me,
then gathering all the feelings up like a rainbow of colours mixed in a pot to one, channelling them into a fine,
laser beam of life-destroying violence. If you control it
and make it positive, victory is yours, if you let it control
you, it will weaken and destroy you. Be master of it, not
factotum to it.

A group of heavy set lads who looked like they'd come
straight off the 'Flintstones' set walked from out of the
precinct towards my car, I scanned the faces to find familiarity. I saw none. They got closer, one looked as
though he was carrying some kind of bat or shotgun, in
the dark and from the distance they were at, I couldn't be
sure. They got closer, was this them, was this a set up? I
gripped the corded handle of my sword and readied
myself to war, the adrenaline flushed through me at a
hundred miles an hour. I felt like I wanted a shit, like I
wanted to run, like I wanted to scream. I held it all to-

gether ready to release it behind my sword . . . my blunt
sword! Bastard. I wished I'd sharpened it now, at this
rate I'd only 'dent' them.

They were right on top of the car now. Should I start
the car and drive off? There were four of them, all ugly as
fuck. Should I drive the car into them? I gripped the inside door handle of my Sierra ready to open it and fight,
I let the adrenaline loose slightly to give myself a little
anger, when they came for me I'd let the lot out like a
rabid monster. This is where it's at, this moment before
engagement when the adrenaline, the fear, reached its
pinnacle and felt like hell, gathering in the cavity of your
chest like a burning fireball of negative emotion that makes
you feel like breaking down in a crying quivering heap of
jellied shit. It rises from your chest to your nasal passage
like toxic gas, gnawing away at you like caustic, tempt-
ing you to crack, daring you to fight, questioning your
ability to 'handle it' telling you to flee, to run, to hide, to
GO! GO! GO!

NO!

You stop it dead in its tracks with a granite will, tempered from a life time of 'will forging' confrontations in
Dojos, Gyms and nightclubs. This is where it's really at,
this single moment before breaks more men than it
doesn't, you have to run with this feeling, accept it, be
one with it, welcome the pain, bath in the anguish, even
invite it in in greater proportions. That's the way to beat
it, but it's hard, fucking hard (harder than four or even
five regular 'hards'), that's why fear is the friend of exceptional people. As Helen Keller said, 'The best way out
is through'.

They walked past my car and down the steps in to the
club. I breathed a deep sigh of relief.

A girl approached my car. She was diminutive and
pretty, with long, gypsy, dark hair and a cute body (I
notice these things). Her black trousers blew in the cool
evening breeze and she pulled a worn mid-length sheep

skin close to her body as protection against the biting wind. She was followed by an older women in a heavy butterfly collared crimplene coat and a heavily flowered hat. Why is it that when women reach fifty they start dressing like Musketeers? I wondered whether she might be carrying a fencer's foil. Up close I noticed that she sported a broken nose, it looked precariously out of place on what was otherwise a gentle, elderly face. Broken faces are a common feature on women married in to 'crime families'. It's so sad because underneath you can usually see a lovely girl or woman just praying to get out, in these kind of environments the men keep the women in place with a hand of iron. One or two that I know personally have been literally crippled for DARING to forget their place.

I got out of my car to greet them, looking all around for the possible set-up. Even my car was parked for a quick getaway.

"Geoff," said the sweet, Scottish voice, she continued without waiting for my reply.

"P was arrested at the pub this morning, so I've come in his place." We shook hands.

"Come and sit in the car," I offered, motioning with my hand towards the car. I was trying to be as nice as possible: I have a lot of respect for ladies and after all, my argument was not with them. I opened the front passenger door for the young girl, my Samurai sword was on the front seat, and I wanted her to see it.

"You should have seen the size of the sword he had with him, P," I knew she would say when she reported back to him.

"Thank fuck I didn't go," I knew he'd reply.

Dartagnon opened the back door of the car and sat in the back seat, the young lady went to sit on the passenger seat.

"AHH!" she shouted involuntarily, nearly dying of shock at the sight of the sword.

"Sorry about that," I lied, as I moved it to make room for her on the seat. The young girl introduced the Musketeer in the back seat as her mother, P's mother. Fucking hell, I was gobsmacked. The man had sent his mother.

"P couldn't come," said the broad, guttural, Scottish voice from the back seat, "he got arrested at the dole this afternoon."

My eyes met with the young girl in the front. She'd said he was arrested in the pub this morning, the mother had just said he was arrested in the dole this afternoon. Basically, this meant he hadn't been arrested at all, he was probably under the table at home searching for his lost bottle. I refrained from mentioning the mishap, things were embarrassing enough already. The mother continued,

"My P doesn't go into houses," she defended, "it's that slag M that he married [call me perceptive but I noted a hint of animosity towards her daughter-in-law]. My boys don't do that, they only rob shops." (Nice boys.)

"I steal from shops," the sister said frankly, "but I never go into houses."

The pride in their words were obvious. Even crooks have some unwritten morals. Dartagnon had the final word, she lifted her shoulders and pushed her chest out as she spoke.

"Yes, I just want you to know that my boys and girl don't do that." And these words were sincere, to them breaking into shops and warehouses was O.K. Because, as they say, 'them type of people can afford it'. Breaking into houses or 'dwellings' as they are commonly known was seen as a low-life crime, unless of course you lived in a posh house then it was different, you fell back in to the 'they can afford it' category again. People who had money, or who had done well for themselves were almost seen as a different race, and it was O.K. to rob them because they have money and as we all know people with money don't have any feelings and deserve everything that they get.

The sister handed me a small, black, velvet purse. She had working hands, cut and callused to match her heart. Our eyes shared a blissful moment, I leaned over and kissed her on the cheek. She smelt nice, and for that split second I felt an affinity with her. Again I felt privileged for being lucky enough to have been brought up without violence and depravation as an education.

I opened up the bag to reveal what I never really expected to see again, my precious gold. I couldn't suppress the smile that creased my face.

"P's a bit worried," said the sister, beginning the bargain that I knew was inevitable.

"Tell him not to worry," I interrupted, "I'm a man of my word. As far as I'm concerned this," I lifted up my bag of gold, "is the end of it. If I see P in the street, I'll say hello to him and bear no grudges, but tell M to keep out of my street. If I see her there again, I'm gonna set my girlfriend on her, she's a black belt and is dying to get into her."

They both gasped at the words 'black belt'. I knew they would.

If I said Sharon was pleased when I returned with the loot, it would be the greatest understatement in the history of the world. She dived all over me and told me I was her hero. (Aw, shucks, I knew that.) The fuss she made was so nice, I contemplated getting a friend to rob our house once a month and me recover the loot once a month, just so she could fuss me again.

The threat of violence in this case was employed, the use of it was, thankfully, not. I see myself as a loaded revolver, sometimes you can get the desired result just by pointing the gun, and not pulling the trigger.

Back home, loot in hand, trouble over, peace restored, the aftermath began. It hit me harder than a tax bill. Aftermath, an explosion of emotions, always comes after adversity, after you have taken your body and mind to their physical and mental limits you often experience a temporary emotional breakdown (some people experience total nervous breakdown after being attacked/raped etc.). If you've been exposed to big build-ups of adrenaline and it isn't released (the physical act, running/fighting etc. releases the adrenaline from the system) as was the case this time. The aftermath is worse, as the body still needs to 'release', its natural release is aftermath. Usually I prepare myself for the aftermath just by expecting it. When you expect something to hit you the impetus of the said strike is lessened. This time, due to the elation of having retrieved my gold without even having to fight I forgot my preparation.

Sharon had gone to visit her nan, I was alone in the house when it started, the depression, the shame, the hate, the worry. I felt like I was dying inside, then the tears, gushing out like Niagara floods, then the absolute shame for crying. What a wanker, crying like a baby, but cry I did for half an hour. I sat in the chair wanting to disappear into its arms. I was beyond comforting, I jumped out of the chair screaming and punched the wall several times until my hands swelled and bled, then I felt ashamed for damaging myself and cried again. I felt like I was dying. I fell from the chair to my knees and sobbed.

3. Face To Face With Death

There are not many doormen who do not, at one time or another, worry about killing somebody. Some worry a little, others a lot. I fall into the last category. I think and worry about it constantly. One of my old school friends was killed in his tender twenties by a doorman, and, just lately, every time you open a newspaper somebody has been killed by a doorman. In my time I have knocked unconscious over fifty opponents whilst 'on duty' and every single time I worried myself sick until they 'came around', and even then worried for a couple of days in case they relapsed into a coma, which seems quite a common occurrence these days. Every time I watch a T.V. programme or film glorifying violence, I think about that overwhelming feeling of fear I get every time I knock somebody out, their pale, chalky, lifeless faces failing to respond to slaps and water douches, and the crowd of whispering onlookers, who you know would hang you should it ever reach court. When they do eventually come around, looking like waking babies, relief is instant and you swear to yourself that you'll never do it again, but you know you will.

'Murder', when you just say it, when you pluck the word out of the air, like a tossed coin, says and means very little: somebody kills someone else. Just a single verb that, until it happens to you or the possibility of it, lays detached from reality, with no real meaning or depth. When you've killed someone, or think you might have, the word becomes frightening and diarrhoea inducing. I've waited, like a prisoner on death row, for many an unconscious foe to come around, watching my own life fall away before my very eyes.

It's not just a case of John killing Fred, John goes to prison, Fred goes to the morgue. Along with John's liberty goes the house he's worked so hard for, his girlfriend/wife who can't wait the twenty year jail term for him, his children's youth, his children! Plus his friends, possibly his family, all his belongings, his self-respect and probably the worst of all, his peace of mind. The list goes on.

Possibly and probably, John loses everything.

When (if) he eventually does come out of jail, he's a broken man, even afraid and unsure of where he stands in the purgatory of the hereafter.

John's family are haunted by the press, ignored by the neighbours, threatened by Fred's family and friends. They become social outcasts, often even taking the blame for what's happened firmly on their own shoulders, the pressure of the extra weight taking years off their lives.

When Fred dies his family are, of course, crestfallen. His young wife has a nervous breakdown from which she never really recovers. Mum cries day and night because the last time she saw Fred, she scalded him for his heavy drinking. His brothers spend the next umpteen years factotum to the negativeness of revenge, the obsession putting pressure on their marriages or relationships and causing arguments, often split-ups.

John's life is over, not just Fred's and both families, who are the real victims, never really recover. Their lives change irreversibly and immeasurably.

Before and during an altercation you don't think of these things, only afterwards does the cold bill of reality drop through the letter-box of your mind.

As you can clearly see, I think about it all deeply, and the constant thought is becoming a great weakness in my alter ego. To be an effective fighter/doorman you have at times to be devoid of such emotions because they cause indecision, and indecision begets defeat, then you become Fred instead of John. Karate teaches, as does life, that you should learn to transcend fighting, it's a sign of maturity in the martial arts, but the same maturity can, as I've mentioned, cause indecision, etc. So, it's a choice between the devil and the deep blue sea. You don't want to fight, but if you don't you'll lose and possibly die. If you do fight you may win but possibly kill. Either way you lose. I've always believed that it's better to be judged by twelve than carried by six. I still hold onto that belief, but only by the skin of my teeth, because killer or killed, your life is over. So, the best way, of course, is to avoid confrontations like the plague, but when violence follows you through life like an unwanted, spotty, bespectacled, little girl on the school playground, as it does every man/ woman who works the door, it's not easy, but we have to try.

D, 'the Karate Kid', as he was commonly known in the Devon pub, due to the fact that he held a black belt in Kung Fu, had barely transcended idiocy, never mind fighting. He was the kind of man that you couldn't dislike . . . until you got to know him.

He saw violence as a romantic might see a lake set in the frame of a dozen mist-topped acres of green foliage. A lot of people who haven't experienced the horrors of real fighting are like this, they romanticise violence imagining a kinship to celluloid fisticuffs, with a hero, a baddie and tomato ketchup blood. When they do 'feel' the real thing it usually appals them, but, until that first 'feel', there's no telling them. As the Chinese say, feeling is believing.

Napoleon Bonaparte once said that there is nothing like the sight of a battlefield after the fight to inspire princes with a love of peace and a hate of war.

The Karate kid had not yet seen his 'battlefield', but the way he was going he would soon, very soon.

He walked like a fighter, talked like a fighter and by golly he knew he was a fighter. He was tall with a lean muscular athletic frame, and handsome features set un-

der a cap of short, dark hair, always five o' clock shadowed (just like the fighters in the movies), and a walk,
what a walk. All he needed were a set of spurs and a six
gun and the picture would be complete. Here was a man
sitting high on the crest of a confidence wave. But, alas,
he was a fool. I was reliably informed that he once had an
arsehole transplant . . . and it rejected him. He walked
with a strutting bounce that made me think he had springs
in his heels, and as was customary with fighters, (I use
the word 'fighter' very loosely), he talked bluntly and
without manners, affording very few a smile. He smacked
of arrogance. (I don't know if it's coming through here,
but I didn't like him very much.)

Having worked the Devon door for two years, I had, of
course, noticed the Karate Kid and sensed his arrogance,
a by-product of overconfidence, but I took little notice of
him. I didn't like him much , and I wasn't alone on that
count, but his way was his prerogative, and if it wasn't
interfering with me or mine, then what the hell was it to
do with me? I did what a fellow worker, an Irish chap
called Seamos (honestly), in Courtaulds many years ago
told me to do with a rather ignorant foreman (weren't
they all), 'took a lot of no notice of him'. That was until
one Tuesday night in cold October, when his over-zealous,
over-confidence, over-flowed into an insult that aimed
itself in my direction.
   Give a man enough rope and he'll hang himself.
   "Would you mind seeing your drinks off, please," I
asked 'the Karate Kid', who was strutting his wares on
the pin-ball machine, he even looked tough doing that.
   "Fuck off, can't you see I'm on the machine?" He
gruffed, without taking his eyes off the game. His tall,
skinny, weasel faced friend, dressed in a scabby black t-
shirt and dirty blue jeans, looking in dire need of a fashion transplant, smiled admiringly, impressed by his
friend's brave comment. He was obviously easily swayed.

"I don't fucking care what ya' doin'," I returned, equally acidic, "just see your drink off." I then turned to his smiling, weaselled compatriot: his smarmy 'fuck off' smile had bothered me lots. "ALRIGHT?" I challenged. Alright, meaning 'if you don't like it, do something about it. He got the message. It reminds me of a time out side B's nightclub many years ago when I'd knocked a chap out cold for calling me a cock sucker (I wouldn't mind but I've never sucked a cock in my life). His mate, obviously upset by his friend's sudden unconsciousness, jumped right in front of me, arms splayed back, chest (what little there was of it) pushed forward, mouth locked in teeth baring pose like a ventriloquist's dummy, his face almost touching mine, the smell of beer off his breath attacking my nasal passages,

"YEA!" he said. That was all, just yea. But that's not what he meant. What that 'street speak' meant translated was,

'That's my mate you've just destroyed there. I'm offended, I feel I have to defend his honour, let's engage in a little fisticuffs my good man,' (or words to that effect).

The word used can be one of many, 'YEA!', 'ALRIGHT!', 'AND!' (followed by a glare, a nod of the head, even a splay of the hands), even 'SO!' All of these single, seemingly meaningless words are actually challenges to engage in a fight. Mostly the word, whichever one it may be, is followed by a physical attack. It's a subliminal action trigger. In the boxing ring the boxer leads with his jab, he uses it to set up the big right, you know this so you learn to parry the jab so as to avoid the right. The street fighter uses dialogue as his leading attack, he uses words like 'yea', 'and' 'so' to set you up for his big right. If you don't understand this then you cannot defend against it and you become just another victim. When you are in the game you learn the language like you might learn French or German in school.

Whilst this was going on, unbeknown to me, Colin, my fellow doorman who was built like a Volvo, was watching the goings on from the office camera. He'd watched me knock out the first one and now stood looking at the silent C.C.T.V. screen as I knocked the second one out (the one who called me 'Yea'). He rushed out of the office to the front door to give me a piece of his mind, his face, black with a Jamaican suntan turned red with rage, he pointed to the two unconscious men on the floor but kept his bulging eyes on me,

"Why did you knock the second one out Geoff?"

I thought for a second, I felt a little silly because 'Yea' as a single word didn't seem enough reason for knocking someone unconscious. I stammered,

"He, well . . . he said . . . he said 'Yea'." It sounded bad. I knew it would.

"You can't 'spark' someone for saying 'Yea'," Colin shouted angrily. I imagined the futility of myself standing in court where the language of 'street' is not known nor understood,

"So, Mr Thompson," the judge would say, "run this one by me again because I'm not sure that I heard you correctly. Why did you knock this man unconscious?"

"Because he said 'Yea', and I don't like people calling me 'Yea'," I would reply, rather unconvincingly. When I finally calmed Colin down I explained to him and he seemed to understand (I think). If you don't know the language and that 'YEA!' 'AND!' 'SO!' etc. will usually be followed by an attack, you'll get hurt. You have to translate what has been said and then attack before they do, but don't expect the judge in county court to understand, he hasn't read the 'real' script, he's only read the edited version that they give you in colleges and schools.

"O.K.," he stammered, swallowing his smile. 'The Karate Kid' remained quiet and carried on playing pinball. I walked away before my temper got the better of me and then him.

"I'm gonna give that wanker a 'car park rash' if he doesn't watch his mouth," I told Alan, my fellow doorman.

Alan laughed, he didn't like him either. Two years ago I'd have probably blasted him into unconsciousness for his ignorance and cheek, but the more mature Geoff let it slip, gave a second chance, held off the sentence, nice chap that I am. I thought with my 'rep' as a half decent Karate man in the city, my friend would have had a little respect for me and give me a wide berth, but he never, silly man.

The atmosphere between us over the next couple of months was almost palpable. Every week I'd ask him politely to 'drink up', he'd politely ignore me like a whiffy subservient. It went on and on, I guess I should have said something and nipped it in the bud, but I was trying to avoid a scene, not because I was scared of him, just because I was desperately trying to gain promotion from the league of violence in which I found myself and I wasn't going to do that by fighting at the drop of a hat. He obviously thought my reluctance was born through fear.

The final, inevitable straw came on a November Sunday evening. The pub was as busy as usual. At the end of the evening, Sundays are notoriously slow to empty, people seem to think that by grabbing onto a few extra moments before closing time they will delay the inevitable Monday morning feeling that awaits them as soon as their heads hit the pillow on Sunday night.

The long lounge room was heaving with people of every age, colour and creed, the bar staff were walking around collecting glasses and wiping tables, trying to squeeze between slow drinking punters. Smoke herded above the heads of all like rising fog, one of the doormen opened the exit doors to let in a little cold (letting in the cold air was a good way of hinting to people that it's 'time to go', also the draft encourages the same) and let out a little smoke. It bellowed out like dry ice smoke on a dance floor. As I walked around I talked and joked with friends and strangers alike, I bent down by the side of a beautiful girl in a wheelchair, once a brilliant athlete paralysed in a freak car accident. I kissed her on the cheek, she blushed and brushed back her silky auburn hair. I hugged her face into mine, she smelt of expensive perfume and roses (I made the roses bit up, I thought it sounded nice).

"You're gorgeous, you are," I told her. She smiled, the two girls and two lads sat with her smiled also.

"You're spoiling me you are," she replied, shyly.

"You need spoiling," I said laughingly as I continued my walk around the pub.

One of the glass collectors, a pretty looking young man with middle parted long brown hair and a Michelle Pfeiffer face, who was always the brunt of our jokes (and us the brunt of his the cheeky little bastard) walked past with hands full of glasses. He nudged in to me,

"Get out of my way you puff!" he said, jokingly. I grabbed him around the neck and started to strangle him, albeit very gently.

"A young man with his hands full shouldn't be so fucking cheeky," I whispered into his ear, then I bit as though I was going to go right through. When he screamed I let him go and started laughing. He got a safe distance away from me and shouted,

"Next time puff!"

I laughed again. The fun with the bar staff and customers was probably my favourite part of the job.

'The Karate Kid' was strutting his wares by the bar with his friends. As usual I asked him to drink up, as usual, he blanked me, and I blanked him, blanking me (blanker). I collected a few glasses and squeezed through the crowds, making my way to the bar to discard them. In a fit of blatant ignorance 'the Karate Kid' stood in my way, blocking my path. For a second I contemplated feeding him a glass, but knew that wouldn't be fair, (some poor barmaid would have to clean up the mess). He nodded his head sardonically, like one of those nodding dogs in the back of a car. I could tell that he didn't care who I was nor what I could do, if I wanted to get to the bar, I'd damn well have to go around him. His chest swelled in his black, cotton, cap sleeve t-shirt, (very Seventies).

'Call yourself a fucking doorman,' he must have thought to himself, 'I could do your job, you're nothing'. (Do I sound paranoid?)

I'd had enough of action man's arrogance so I pushed him out of my way with my shoulder. Immediately I felt his angry eyes burning into the back of my head as I passed him on my way to the bar. I smiled nervously to myself. On the way back from the bar he stood in my way again. I felt like hitting him with a right hook but settled for the shoulder push again. I barged him out of my way and his eyes nearly popped out of their sockets. As I strolled away from him, I turned and smiled as if to say,

"What the fuck are you gonna do about that, then?" My stomach began its customary, pre-fight churn as my paranoid, over-active adrenal gland went into action. I kept my face even, so as not to show him my build-up. He showed everyone his by staring holes in me, straightening his back, retracting his shoulders, and expanding his chest, his fists clenched and unclenched in a blatant display of immaturity and unprofessionalism. I could tell he hadn't done much by this display, but that didn't stop him from being potentially dangerous. I knew now that there was going to be a lot of trouble and it was my own fault for not stopping this thing when it first started. It's always the same, though, you give a man an inch and he'll take a mile.

Well, I was sick of him now, he'd pushed me too far: he was going to have to have some. I couldn't be too careful though, he was a black belt, and apparently he was quite good. Alan, big at five ten and fourteen stone, with short greying dark hair and a handsome face, listened as

I told him about the incident. As we spoke I noticed out of the corner of my eye that 'the Karate Kid' had collared Seymour, the head doorman. They talked a moment urgently, then looked my way.

"Sort it out, hey Sey'," I heard 'the Karate Kid' say aggressively as they parted. Seymour approached Alan and I. He was an excellent doorman with many years of experience lying in his wake. Who this man had not fought in his time was not worth talking about. He was also a real gentleman. Immaculately smart with heavy gold jewellery and Omega watch, his roguish Jamaican face centred by the perfunctory broken nose, the badge of battle hereabouts, he leaned in towards Alan and myself.

"Have you had any trouble with D?" he asked us both, in a concerned voice. My adrenaline went in to overdrive, this was it.

"Yea. I 'ave Sey', why, wot's 'e said?"

Seymore shrugged his shoulders and grimaced.

"He didn't actually say it was you, Geoff, but he was talking 'fighting talk'." Seymore's voice fell into Jamaican slang at the end of each sentence, especially when fighting was mentioned.

"Does he want to 'speak' to me then, Sey?" I said, knowing the answer before I asked.

"Yea, I think so," came the expected reply. As soon as Sey spoke I went into fight mode, every one and everything disappeared outside the periphery of my tunnel vision. I walked toward the open, exit doors where he was standing like a proud cock with his mate the weasel and a couple of young ladies. My adrenaline rose higher, but I had no problem controlling it because I was so PISSED OFF. I was so angry that this fucking wanker was forcing me to employ physical tactics when I was so desperately trying to elevate myself from the mighty clutch of violence. You see my problem is that I can take a lot of shit and hold myself back quite well, but (and this is a big but, as big as three ordinary buts), when I 'go' I really do 'go', and I find it hard to stop myself. This lack of control will one day get me into a lot of trouble. What was about to happen was so unnecessary. He'd placed me in a position now where I had to fight. If I didn't I would lose 'face' badly, 'face' being other people's respect for you. This is your power base as a doorman: every time you let someone off for a disrespectful act it chips away at your power base. Let it happen too often and you no longer have a power base. Without it you can't do the job you're paid to do because people won't let you if they have no respect. This lack of respect is so contagious, if one person talks to you like shit the next thing you know everyone is trying it on. I've seen it happen again and again, and not just on the door, in every walk of life. It's like the teacher in school that lets one kid off for not doing his homework, the next thing you know half the class stop doing the homework; the teacher who punishes the lazy student gets all his homework in on time. What do you do with a puppy or a kitten to stop them wetting on the carpet? You rub their nose in it. In the great book 'Papillon' the governor of one of the jails that he attended publicly executed the first man that tried to escape from his prison. If he didn't, everyone would be trying to escape at every given chance. I was about to rub a puppies nose into the pile in the hope that he would stop 'pissing on my carpet'.

Several other people looked on as I moved closer to 'the Karate Kid'. My adrenaline reached fever pitch. He was fidgeting on the spot and nodding his head, breathing heavily and staring right through me. These were all the effects of adrenaline; an experienced fighter would never let them show.

"You wanna speak wi' me?" I said in an angry voice.

"Yea, I do actually," he returned evenly.

"Come out here, then," I beckoned as I walked a few feet into the car park. He followed without demur, like a lamb to the slaughter. As he approached he began to angle his body sideways, as though he was lining me up with a kick, though I couldn't be sure. It mattered not as I'd already decided to hit him anyway. I'd spent two months trying to avoid it and was fed up with trying, I had no more chances left in my 'chance' bag.

As he got closer his face began to grimace and I sensed a strike at any moment.

'BANG!' Almost in slow motion, I hooked my right fist onto his advancing jaw, pushing it backward, shaking his grey matter into the realms of unconsciousness. As he fell, I volleyed his face and he spiralled, like movie strobe. I kicked him so hard that it hurt my foot. I felt hate leaving my body: he landed face down and forlorn on the cruel, black tarmac of defeat. Many people were watching, so I thought I'd give them a display, not for exhibitionism, nor fun, nor ego, I just wanted to take out a little insurance, making the onlookers think that I was an animal would, in the future, insure that they did not tangle with me. It's what the Chinese call killing a chicken to train a monkey (slaughtering a live chicken in front of a monkey that they were trying to train).

"Kiaaa," I screamed as I brought an axe kick onto the body of my sleeping quarry. To the onlooker, it probably looked barbaric, (which is how I wanted it to look), but in reality, the kick was empty, I pulled it on impact, just as I had thousands of times before in training.

The man with the weasel face ran at me with ill-intent and I stopped him in his tracks with a lash of my tongue.

"GER OUT 'F MY FUCKING FACE BEFORE I DE-STROY YA!"

He stopped in his tracks like an insect on fly paper. The crowd of onlookers murmured, Seymour tried to pick 'the Karate Kid' off the floor where he lay like yesterday's litter. As I walked past, his face was about waist height, so I back heeled it, again just for show. It had the desired effect because, as I re-entered the pub, somebody shouted,

"Fucking animal!" (flatterer). Several glances met mine as I walked through the doors, disdain painted all over them. The beautiful lady in the wheelchair gave me a look of disappointment. I shrugged my shoulders. Kenny, the body builder, joined the several desperately trying to find 'the Karate Kid's' lost consciousness, (it was obviously very well hidden, because no-one seemed to be able to find it). I watched from the door with horror as the cadaver-like lump of body refused to move.

'Wake up you bastard,' I cried inside, 'wake up.'

My nightmare had begun.

Several would-be first aiders tried, to no avail, to bring him around. I'm sure he was pretending so as to worry me shitless. It was beginning to work, because my bowels churned and threatened to desert me. I held onto them by clenching the cheeks of my bum and vowing never to eat a curry before work again. Kenny, a pocket Hercules, with short, ginger hair, and a permanent smile, moved in to have a go.

'Good,' I thought, 'Kenny will get him round, he's done this loads of times.' No. 'The Karate Kid' was having none of it. His companions were beginning to panic, talking of hospitals and police and other such un-niceties. In the end, three of them picked him up, still unconscious, and carried him to a waiting car, the toes of his shoes dragged and scuffed across the car park. He definitely didn't look healthy.

The orange Mini that held him sped from the car park, leaving me hanging from the ceiling by my finger nails. I felt certain in my mind that he was dead, and by the look on Kenny, Alan and Seymour's faces, they thought so too. I shook my head.

'Why the fuck did I kick him? Why didn't I just knock him out and leave it at that?'

If you kill somebody with a single punch, you may have some chance of defence in court, but if you kicked him as well, especially whilst he was unconscious, you had no chance. So many witnesses too. I thought about Sharon at home in bed, her supple warmth beckoning me, and suddenly, I had to be with her. A shadow darkened over my heart and I felt very low, I had to go home to Sharon, to hold her, be with her. If he's dead, what will I do? How will she cope? She'll lose the house, there's no way she could afford to keep it alone.

Alan lay sleeplessly on his pine, double bed, his brown, sinewy muscled body glistened in the moonlight that stole through the window of his third floor Woodend flat. Al felt sure that 'the Karate Kid' was dead . . . and it bothered him. He'd seen unconscious people before, but not like this, no blood or gore, but . . . he just looked dead. His face was blue and his body jellified, he must have been out ten minutes before they took him to hospital. He knew I was going to take him out, (not for dinner), he deserved it too, (not dinner), he just wished that Geoff, the hair trigger, hadn't been quite so severe. I was Al's best friend, so he was destined to share my sleeplessness.

Kenny lay on the single bed in his own room at his mother's terraced house half way down a tree-lined street in Wyken, a nicer part of the city. He could have slept but saw no point, he was pretty sure he was going to be arrested tonight. After all, he was one of the last people to touch the 'body'. Ken had seen hundreds of unconscious people and had, in his time, become a bit of a 'whiz' at bringing them around, but not 'the Karate Kid'. He'd told me at the time he thought the K. K. was alright, just to ease my mind. Secretly he believed 'the Karate Kid' was in a bad way, as bad at least as any he'd seen in all of his eight years on the door.

He breathed in a deep sigh, almost smacking himself in the face with his huge rooster chest. I had, in all the years I'd known Ken, never seen him without a smile on his face. He looked like Batman's 'the joker'. Ken, who was bigger sideways than he was in height, was one of the most respected doormen in the city, also one of the biggest wind-up merchants in the city too. If you let him he'd have you in tears, telling you that your girlfriend was sleeping around, or that you're looking fat when you're trying to lose weight, thin when you're trying to gain weight, or the good looking girl you fancy is a 'tramp' with more conquests than Chris Bonnington.

"She's nice Ken," you'd say, pointing to a good looker in the corner of the pub.

"She's a 'tramp'," he'd tell you, matter of factly, then reel of a list of men who'd slept with her. And it didn't matter who you were, if you were in the company you'd be having some.

At twelve-thirty a.m. the front door knocker on Kenny's house nearly had him jumping out of his skin. He ran and looked out of the bedroom window.

SHIT! There was a copper waiting at the door.

As I drove back along the deserted streets to my house I pondered on what a lonely place the world could be. I thought too about the mess I was in and the bigger mess my life would become if 'the Karate Kid' popped his socks. I was living a nightmare. In court I wouldn't stand a maggot on a hook's chance of surviving, everything was against me. Although I had only done what I had to do and lived by the laws of the concrete jungle I knew that I would die a death in the law of the court room which was black and white with very few grey areas. In my job life is a jungle, but as someone once said, all the animals are wearing 'people suits', when the witnesses against me appeared in court they would, no doubt, be wearing their very best 'people suits'.

Trying to satisfy a judge that I was innocent would be like trying to convince a white mouse that a black cat was lucky. I had more chance of nailing jelly to the ceiling.

I pulled into the cul-de-sac where my house lay quiet like a sleeping kitten. I parked the car, made my way up the garden path and in to the temporary sanctuary of my home. I didn't expect to be here for long before I was arrested.

Kenny opened the bedroom window slightly, preparing himself to hear the bad news. He was sure now that he was about to be arrested. From the top the policeman's head looked like a huge tit: Kenny wondered if his head went right to the top of it. The door was still not answered, he knocked again more determinedly.

Sharon was in bed when I got home, sometimes she waited up for me, other times, if she was really tired, she'd go upstairs and fall asleep watching the portable telly. I made my way up the stairs and entered the bedroom. She was snugly tucked under the covers like a little baby, the whole room was a glow of fervent memories and warmth. I felt a tug on my heart: was this the end? Was I going to lose her after tonight, forever because of a wanker they called 'the Karate Kid'? (I doubted whether he would keep that name for much longer after tonight's debacle, perhaps they might change it to the 'crappy' kid?)

I lay, still clothed, on the bed next to Sharon. I could smell her white musk perfume, feel the radiating warmth emitting from her body, sense the helplessness she would taste when I was gone. Prison to someone as close as us would be akin to death.

Now, I lay next to my beautiful, smooth skinned, lovely Sharon; tomorrow I could be sharing a bunk with a farting, burping, hairy arsed malefactor with a face like a caveman's ugly club and stinky, polluting breath. The thought made me shudder. I cuddled up to my lady, she half awoke and held me tight. What the fuck had I done?

My body craved sleep, but alas my bed was one of nettles (I'd made my bed, now I had to lie on it, I know, I know) and my mind had gone into overdrive, so there was little chance. I kissed Sharon gently on her soft lips (aren't they always that much softer when you think you're kissing them for the last time?) and ran my fingers softly through her dark, short, soft hair. I wondered whether this would be the last time I'd get to do this.

Her tired eyes opened to greet me then closed again involuntarily, making her look much younger than her twenty-one years, and vulnerable, gosh she looked so vulnerable. Who would take care of her when I was away, who would make her laugh, cradle her to sleep at night, love her, need her? (All my mates would probably be queuing up when I was out the way, mates are like that.) She needed me. She was independent and strong, but I knew she'd grown to need me, even a day apart saw us hugging and kissing on reunion as though a year had passed by.

I thought of my beautiful children who doted on me. Kerry who spent hours late at night conversing with me on anything and everything. Lisa, beautiful Lisa, who loved to jog with me at weekends, hit the ball in my garage gym and push hands when the others were watching telly. Jennie, the others call her 'the leach', because she never leaves my side, following me everywhere, and not really talking, just linking onto me, holding me. Then there was Louis, whose wavy, blond hair, deep, cavernous blue eyes and red, chubby face enchanted me, and his constant barrage of three year old's questions,

"Why, daddy, why?" was his reaction to every question you answered. How would they be without me, and me without them?

Lying there, the similarity to waiting on death row was uncanny. The transfiguration from liberty to lock-up was, to me, life to death. Life without Sharon, without my kids, without my freedom, was, leastways, definitely not 'life'. To assuage my fears I tried to convince myself that 'the Karate Kid' was alright and indeed not D.O.A., but the omniscient Mr Negative inside me was having none of it. I wasn't about to get off that easy.

I decided, as I always do in situations like this, that if I was going to come to terms with what I'd done and the possible consequences, and thus get a little sleep, I was going to have to come to terms with and accept those consequences. The only way to do this was to ask myself what was the worst possible thing that could happen in this situation? Then answer myself honestly. I could go to prison.

I then put my mind into the highest gear it will go into and tell myself that, 'I can handle that'. If the worst comes to the worst, he dies and I inevitably go to prison, 'I could handle it'.

Your mind is a funny old tool, enmeshed at times of stress with negativeness, always looking on the black side of things, worrying, nagging, destroying your will, so that it has the complete control it wants. When control is gained it destroys the body with ulcers, tumours, heart attacks, strokes, nervous breakdowns, giving in to your own mind is, effectively, like pulling the plug on life. The brain is like the proverbial 'school bully', the body, the bespectacled, thin bookworm on whom he preys. The more the bookworm gives in to the bully, the more powerful and dominant the bully becomes, until the bully burgeoning on the weakness completely devours the boy . . . and he is no more. (Well, at least my mind is like that.)

I gently shook Sharon to wake her up, then unbosomed myself to her, telling her that I expected to be arrested that night, and that she should be strong, and that, if she had any strength to spare could I have it? She nodded her assent sleepily and I cradled her off to sleep.

My imagination wandered as sleep beckoned, I found myself cuffed to a 'rozzer' entering a conceptual, echoey court room, where 'the Karate (crappy) Kid's' friends and family stood in judgment as judge, jury and executioner, pointing and moaning in haunting voices, 'Animal! Animal! Animal! And I, dressed in a pantomime wolf's head and sheep's clothing, stood in the dock trying to convince an old fart of a judge, whose epitome of violence was a 'biff' on the nose in a public school playground, then shake hands and be 'jolly good friends' afterwards, and 'gosh Nigel, wasn't it a wheeze', that knocking a man unconscious then doing a fifty-six move Kata on his head was justifiable, and that, 'I never really kicked him hard, your honour, I pulled the kicks on impact, they where only for show'.

The judge, answered with a perfunctory shake of the head, and a thumbs down. The smiling policeman (the one wearing the same bracelet as me) whose clothing suddenly changed to those of the grim reaper with a little badge on the chest that said 'KARMA', led me 'down the steps'. The judge, the jury and the gallery laughing theatrically in unison as I am led away, I look up to the gallery as I am almost out of sight to see my mates hovering around and touching a tearful Sharon.

'UUHH!' I woke up with a start in a cold sweat. I thought for a moment about the courts and Judges.

I know someone has to rule this fair land of ours, and I understand that they should, for obvious reasons, be educated, but why are they always so detached from reality, they have absolutely no conception of the 'real world', the one outside of the court room. They know not the language nor the body talk of 'street', and that when someone hostile says 'YEA!' they mean 'Yea, do you wanna go' or if they splay their hands erratically, lurch their neck forward like a pecking hen, or turn side ways on to you it means that they are preparing to attack. Or that when a good fighter says that he doesn't want to fight you it means that he does want to fight you, he's just disarming you before engagement. If he smirks and nods his head he's subliminally calling you a wanker. If you ask him to 'leave the club' or 'behave' and he doesn't answer, or worse still if he very slowly looks you up and down and then doesn't answer, he's telling you that he respects you so little that you don't even warrant a reply, and 'you're a piece of shit'. There are so many ways that a person can throw the gauntlet without actually saying 'let's fight' and each in its own right demanding a response if 'face' is to be saved , but try and explain this to a judge or jury who doesn't understand 'street speak' and who are 'out there with Pluto'.

"You say that you hit this fellow because he nodded his head Mr Thompson? Pray show me the book that details the language of which you speak."

These people have no conception of real life or the trappings of a working class whose unwritten scripture says 'if you don't fight, if you can't fight, you're fucked'.

I remember the time my brother Gary was in court for fighting many years ago, his opponents, as coincidence would have it, doormen from Birmingham. The one particular chap Gary got tangled with was a giant of a man at twenty-five stone and built like Wembley Stadium. One of Gary's witnesses pointed the monster out in court saying,

"It was definitely him, I'll never forget him because he reminded me of the Incredible Hulk." The judge, who everybody thought was asleep, dead or mannequined, suddenly shot his head to attention.

"Incredible Hulk?" he said, mystified, and to no one in particular. The defence counsel (he had obviously done his homework) interjected,

"Fictional character, off television, m'Lud."

The judge looked baffled,

"Oh! Carry on counsel," he muttered.

What is wrong with this movie? Anyway, I digress, I'd got my head around prison, but sleep was still eluding me. My ears seemed to prick like an alert Alsatian, picking up every sound and movement like a radio antenna. I could hear Sharon's soft breathing, the clang of the central heating, the distant call of motorway car engines, the hum of nearby electricity cables, even the thumpety thump of my own heartbeat was starting to 'cabbage' me.

Fuck me, I wanted to shout to all the inanimate objects,

'Can't you see I'm trying to sleep?' I desperately listened for the crack of police boots on the paving slabs of my footpath, (bastards, all those biscuits and coffees I'd given them over the years, as well), or the ring of the phone saying,

'He's dead, he's dead, he's dead'.

The fluttering leaves of the conifers that I tended so lovingly, joining in unison with the wind,

'He's dead, he's dead, he's dead,' (that's the last time I cut and trim you, you bastards).

Then, the very neighbour's cat that I left saucers of milk for, getting all his mates in my garden,

'Miaow, he's dead, he's dead, miaow,' (there'll be cyanide in your milk tomorrow).

'KNOCK', HUH! I awoke with a start. Was that the door?

The policeman stood waiting at Kenny's door, the tension was killing Ken, he contemplated shouting his mum to 'Answer the bloody door will you', but he didn't need to. The door was opened, his mother greeted the awaiting policeman.

"Sorry to bother you, Madame. Is that your Cortina?" He pointed to a beige car on the roadway outside the house. Kenny's mum looked, so did Ken.

"No, it belongs to the Campbells next door."

"No problem, he's left his side lights on, that's all. I'll give him a knock, save his battery."

'PHEW!' Thank fuck for that,' Kenny thought as he jumped back into bed.

I sat up with a jerk, woken by the knock, from the restless sleep where nature condemned me. Was that the door?

The police? A friend delivering bad news? Was that loud knock my 'coup-de-grace'? I looked at the time on the electric clock on the small bedside table beside Sharon. There was no clock, a thought came into my head. If my clock was made of cloth would time be immaterial? (In material, get it?) The clock lay forlorn and upturned on the carpet where Sharon had rolled in her sleep and knocked it off. I wanted to shout, 'you clumsy bastard', but decided best not.

I tried to recapture the lost sleep, if I could last the night without being arrested, I'd be home free (if you'll forgive the pun). If he was dead or comatose, I'd have been arrested by now. I unashamedly clasped my hands and prayed to God for forgiveness and a fifty-first chance. Sleep overcame me, and almost a second later, morning arrived. As soon as I awoke the previous night's fears were back, perched on the shoulder of my mind's eye like a hungry vulture, but to a slightly lesser degree. I'd survived the night without arrest, which was a good sign.

All the same, I switched my radio on to local Mercia for the news, then Harmony for their news, then CWR. When bad news was not forthcoming, (gladly), I switched to Radio One to see if 'Batesy' had heard anything. Apparently not. Sharon gave me plenty of comforting hugs, telling me it would be alright. After I'd dropped her off at work, I decided to go and see Al. He'd put my mind at rest.

"I thought he was dead Geoff." (Well maybe not).

Seeing the dismay his words had caused he retreated,

"Though I'm sure he's not, you'd have heard by now." (Too late, Al, the damage is done.) Though he did say 'the Karate Kid' was a wanker and needed some pain (I knew that) which helped to assuage my mind a little.

We switched on the telly for a bit of light relief only to find that every channel was platforming talks, plays and films about violence and death, displaying vignettes of

brutality and going into the histrionics of how easy somebody could be killed by a kick to the head. The BBC and
Central T.V. seemed, like nature the night before, to be
ganging up on me, and it wasn't fair.

Coventry city arcade became a wind tunnel as a northerly
gust ran through it like an icy gauntlet, blowing anything
and everything this way and that, except my hair, which
was tightly concealed under my leather Fila hat. I hadn't
much hair left due to hereditary receding, one good gust
of wind and I could be completely bald, and we don't
want that. The arcade held a scattering of only the gallant
(or stupid) who dared to brave the winter chill.

I made my way to the end of the arcade where the
'paper man' stood, his eyes hidden amidst a thousand
wrinkles, mouth lost in a Walrus moustache and head
veiled under a chequered, ill-fitting cap that met and
matched the turned up lapels of an overcoat that went
right to his toes like heavy curtains, sweeping the floor as
he walked, he looked like one of those wool dolls that
your mum made you when you were little. Every now
and then his mouth would emerge from its hiding place
under the uncut 'tache (that sported a bit of uneaten pie
in the left corner) like a gaping hole in a walker's welly.

"AAUUU!" came his completely and utterly inaudible sales pitch, which, roughly translated, meant, 'Telegraph'. Or if it was an evening edition of the paper,
"CIIFO!" which meant (yes you've guessed it) 'City Final'. There were about ten of these lovely characters scat-
tered all around the city centre, selling the splendid 'Coventry Evening Telegraph' from portable kiosks. They were
all uniform in their nondescript attire and decimation of
the English language. I wondered whether a) the skill was
passed down to them from past sellers, b) if it was just
natural, or c) because of the pedantic nature of the job,
whether they'd included the 'language' as an exciting
pastime. Anyway, I bought twenty-five pence worth of

'AAUUU', to see if I was headlining or whether my imagination was just playing a cruel, cruel, not funny joke on me.

I scanned every page. My heart jumped when I saw the headline, 'Local Man Murdered'.

I read the headline story as quickly as I could, in between gusts of wind blowing the pages into my eyeline, my hands shaking like a boy cat at the neuter clinic. I stumbled over the words scanning for my name, hoping it wasn't there.

It wasn't me. I threw my head back in relief, it wasn't me. It was someone murdered in a domestic incident in neighbouring Bedworth (gosh, that'll bring the population down to twenty-one). I sat in my neat, clean, furnished front room staring at the telephone like it was a sizzling joint of lamb, and I was on a 'no lamb' diet. I wanted to pick it up and ring the Devon to see if they'd heard anything, but I daren't. What if they had and it was 'bad'? That was the last thing I wanted to hear. On the other hand, it could be good news. I decided to ring, I'd have to find out sooner or later. The dull tring at the end of my earpiece seemed to go on forever. Every ring sent waves down to my churning, clenching stomach, 'ring, ring, ring, ring', a paroxysm of anticipation consumed my whole being. My bottom was doing the dance of a thousand 'run runs'. 'Come on you bugger, answer the fucking phone.' I was talking to myself again, it was getting worrying. My Doctor told me that I was a schizophrenic, but we just laughed at him.

"Hello?" came the quiet, unassuming, disembodied voice at the other end of the line, it was Jim, our diffident, gentleman boss at the Devon pub.

"Hello Jim, it's Geoff." There was a cold silence. "Have you heard anything?" I asked hopefully.

"Well," he said, pausing momentarily, prolonging my agony, "hold on a minute Geoff, let me take the call in my office, hold on a sec'."

The distance between the bar and the office was, at the most, five feet, so why did it take Jim three hours and twenty minutes to get there? Why? Time distortion, that's why. I don't know what I've ever done to offend this omniscient tactician of pain, but I must have done something very bad because he certainly had it in for me. Eventually Jim came back on the line.

"He hasn't been in Geoff, but as far as I can tell, he's alright, one of the locals said he'd seen him out and about."

Radiant relief filled my stress-torn body.

"One of the locals 'as seen him, you say?" I asked, wanting the good news re-affirming, in case my ears deceived me.

"Yea, anyway, you'd have heard by now if he wasn't," he said as an after-thought.

If I was brothers with stress, I was definitely sleeping with relief, because it did feel nice.

'Yippee!' I wanted to shout, so I did, but felt a right twat afterwards and decided not to do it again, less the neighbours think I'd lost my marbles.

In the spacious porchway of the Devon, looking in to the lounge out on to the large car park that held only a light peppering of cars, Alan, Kenny, Seymour and I laughed and joked about how we were all sure 'the Karate Kid' was dead (it wasn't so funny at the time) and how our imaginations had run wild.

"He was in earlier on, Geoff," Kenny said. "Well, I say he was 'in', he wouldn't get out of the car, he was shitting himself in case you battered him again. He was as nervous as fuck, he asked whether you were in yet, I told him you'd be in later."

"I'm just fucking glad he's not dead."

All the lads laughed, they shared my relief, they'd all been there before. Kenny continued,

"I told him you wouldn't do anything, Geoff. I 'ad to, he looked like he was gonna cry." We all laughed again.

About an hour later the Karate Kid drove into the car park in a battered purple Capri. He wound the window down, I was stood by the door. Even from here I could see his supplication, it was almost tangible.

His voice was capitulating.

"Can I have a word with you please?"

"Yea, sure." I could see that he was scared and I didn't want to tear the arse out of it so I put him at ease by talking nicely. This is my way. There's a temptation in cases like this to rub salt in to the wound; when you've beaten someone it's almost as though they are in your power. If you say 'jump', they say 'how high?' A lot of the lads would have battered him again, or at the very least employed intimidating verbal, because they enjoy the feeling of power over another human being. They can't resist bullying, and at the end of the day that's all it is, bullying. No matter what someone has done to you, once the punishment has been administered that should be the end of it, unless they push it any further. I don't like the feeling of 'people domination', when I beat someone I always feel sorry for them, hurting people hurts me deep inside, though I do enjoy it at the time: not because I'm sadistic, nor because I like hurting people, I'm not and I don't. It's the fact that I've 'held it' and the fact that I've survived that feels good, the endomorphines that the body releases after exertion (fighting, training, surviving etc.) gives you the natural high that makes you feel good, almost a reward for having the bottle to 'dare' and the ability to survive. The guilt and apathy I feel after the fight, though, put me on a low that is a lot lower than the high is high. My greatest high comes from helping people, making people feel good, making people happy. Those who do not understand the 'power' and misuse it usually drift to the dark side, this has happened to some of my friends.

"Sorry about the other night," he offered, looking at the floor.

"Forget it, it's done. I'm not a man to hold a grudge, as far as I'm concerned it's over."

"I didn't think it had gone that far," he continued, "I didn't want any trouble with you, I knew who you were, the last thing I wanted was trouble."

"Well, why two months ago did you tell me to 'fuck off' when I asked you to see your drink off?"

"I didn't mean it like that."

"How many ways am I supposed to take 'fuck off'?"

He shrugged his shoulders.

"And ever since then you've gone out of your way to be disrespectful, standing in my way when I was collecting the glasses, ignoring me when I ask you to drink up. I mean, what am I supposed to think?"

He shrugged again.

"I'm sorry." He paused. "Am I barred? All my mates drink in here, I'd hate to be barred."

I patted him on the arm sympathetically,

"As far as I'm concerned, it's forgotten, you can come back into the pub and we can be friends." His eyes lit up like a child receiving a present, his bombastic alter ego crushed.

"Really? I'd like that," he said.

We parted on a handshake and I sighed deeply and thought.

'There but for the grace of God, go I.'

4. Three Card Bluff

You can call someone's bluff once, and if you're lucky and cheeky, even twice, but three times is just taking the piss.

'Mr R' had fallen for my bluff twice. Considering that he was a ribald, violent man, who'd made a career of hurting people and had been an instrument of pain wherever he went, I was more that a little surprised the first two times.

The first time I called his bluff was in the late Eighties, when violence in Coventry pubs was the norm and I was at my aggressive best. Basically, I asked him to leave an establishment, as he held a life ban for petrol bombing the place a couple of years earlier (detailed in 'Watch My Back'). He refused. I challenged him to a fight, he backed down and left. The second time was four years later, not long after he'd been released from jail for much violence and aggravation. Again, I found myself in a position where I had to ask him to leave an establishment in which I was working, different from the first place but for the same reason. He had a life ban, in fact he was so violent that he carried life bans from most of the pubs and clubs in Coventry, the only ones that didn't ban him were the places where the landlords were too scared to do so.

As I'd bluffed him the first time I thought I'd try the same ploy again, after all, at sixteen stone, he was a bit of a monster, so fighting if at all possible was best avoided.

The Lion, a grand Edwardian pub sat proudly in its own large car park just off a main city road, in the popular and quiet Walsgrave. It was a Coventry suburb, with a lovely, picturesque, old, castle-like church to its immediate right, whose tree-darkened graveyard had done nicely, thank you, for many late night lovers who worried not about 'coming' to life in a graveyard, if you'll forgive the pun.

Bill, or Willmot Brown, as the regulars called him on account of his extreme uncanny likeness to the famous, nay infamous villain in the popular soap, Eastenders, who was/is a lovely man, who you just couldn't help but like, was temporarily in charge of the 'Lion' on account of the previous gaffer's inaccuracies with the weekly till rolls (one for the brewery, one for me, one for the brewery, one of me). I was working at the Devon at the time but because I liked Bill and because I knew that he wasn't a fighter, I promised to 'look after him' for his short duration at the pub.

"Any trouble Bill, just ring me and I'll sort it out for you," I told him. Of course, when you make this kind offer, no matter how well meaning it is, you never really expect to be taken up on it.

Sunday afternoon, with a lovely cooked dinner sitting comfortably in the pit of my stomach, I sat on my commodious settee and readied myself for an afternoon of 'eye exercising' on the telly.

The phone rang (as it does when you least want it to).

"Let the answer machine take it, Geoff," shouted Sharon, who was washing up the dinner dishes in the kitchen (I couldn't have washed them as I was far to comfortable). I might have done if it were switched on, but it wasn't, so I picked up the phone.

I knew there was trouble because Bill always gave a big sigh before he gave you the bad news, he sounded worried on the other end of the line.

"'Mr R's' in, Geoff, I've asked him to leave but he won't."

I cursed myself for not having had the answer machine on.

"O.K.," I said, hiding the build-up of adrenaline, "I'm on my way."

When I got there, there was a police car already outside. Someone must have rung them, though nobody knew who. Bill was talking to one of them. I hoped, as I left the comfort and safety of my car, that my knuckle duster swinging at the bottom of my pocket wasn't too obvious. Apparently, 'Mr R' was in the bar with four others, so an equaliser was necessary, just in case.

"Geoff's gonna get him out," Bill confidently told the police, who seemed keen to get in there themselves. They hated him too and saw him as an unreprievable, recalcitrant bastard, who should be in a permanent state of 'lockup'. He had, in his time, demolished several officers of the law, so was very low on their popularity list, though on this lovely Sunday afternoon in February, when I should have been at home, wallowing and being fussed by my lady, he was much lower on mine. I got my head into fight mode, and gnarled up my face in readiness for my confrontation.

Aggressively, I pushed through the double doors and into the pub, which was just one huge room with a circular bar right in the centre, pool tables to the left. To the extreme right, the D.J. council, rising regally, several feet upon a carpet platform, tables and chairs and indeed all space was taken up by a huge amount of Sunday morning drinkers whose eyes all dropped on to me as I burst in. 'Mr R' sat between four hard-faced associates, on a run of red leather seating against the wall and behind three tables of drinks. Alcohol, the force that drove these irksome people.

'Mr R' looked up at me, as did his followers. I met each stare individually with an acerbic counter stare that none could match. I drilled holes in them with my eyes: none met the challenge. All eyes dropped to the table like a bad hand of cards. I'd psyched myself into an aggressive state and would balk at none.

I looked at 'Mr R', his hard, dark face capped by a crown of thick, black hair, his small, fat nose underlined by a thick, black moustache (if I had a nose like that I wouldn't underline it). My extreme show of confidence and scowling face obviously deluged him completely because he accepted my invitation to leave the premises effusively when I whipped the leather, baseball cap off my head in an aggressive, challenging manner. He left almost without demur. The whole establishment sighed a relief as he went, I enjoyed a celebration bottle of beer. This was the second and I hoped the last confrontation with 'Mr R'.

The next four weeks saw a 'Mr R'-free Lion, and, temporarily, I forgot all about him.

Sharon had been poorly all week with a stomach bug that saw her emptying anything and everything that entered her stomach, from both ends. All my family had, over the last couple of weeks, had the bug, so I concluded, rightly so, that diarrhoea 'runs in your genes'. Anyway, by the Thursday, her appetite was returning and her stomach was being a little less fussy, and not catapulting food out as soon as it came in, so I, as a little treat for my lady, cooked a lovely spaghetti for us both. It went down very well (and stayed down) and as I rested on the settee in a bid to let the food siphon from my stomach into my system before the over-filled former burst at the seams. I felt like a pregnant woman (but where the hell was I going to find one this time of the day?).

It was early on the Thursday evening when, 'BRRRR, BRRRR'. The phone buzzed into life (it was a cold phone).

"Let the answer machine take it," said Sharon (in the kitchen again doing some domestic engineering) as she always did.

'Bastard', it wasn't on again.

"Hello?" I said, trying at the same time to watch 'The Bill' on the television out of the corner of my eye, trying to pick up a few tips. The heavy sigh told me that it was

Bill and that it was trouble, the spaghetti turned over in my stomach like a spun cocktail.

"Our friend's back," said the worried Bill on the other end of the line, "and he's got a friend with him, some Scotch guy from Woodend."

"Is anyone else there?" I asked, meaning the other doormen.

"I phoned Les, he said to ring you."

"O.K., is he on his way down?"

"Yea, I think so."

"O.K., I'll be down in a minute."

Sharon looked across the room at me.

"Trouble?" she asked. I shrugged my shoulders and nodded.

"It's that fucking 'Mr R' again, 'e's in the Lion and 'e won't leave."

"Where are the other doormen, Geoff? It's a Thursday night, they must have doormen on."

It was a valid point, but I didn't know the answer. I shrugged again.

"There can't be any on or 'e wouldn't 'ave rung me."

I sat down and tied tightly the shoelaces of my leather, Fila trainers. My fighting shoes. Adrenaline shot into the unexpected mass of spaghetti Bolognaise still digesting in my stomach. I wondered whether I might be seeing it again, very soon.

I decided to try and bluff him again, but I knew in my heart of hearts that this time he wouldn't go for it, this time we'd be fighting. I zipped up my black, Fila tracksuit top and put on my dark, baseball cap which had the initials G.T. embroidered in yellow across the top. My hands shook with adrenaline overload as I zipped up my tracksuit top. I walked to the front door to leave, Sharon jumped up from her seat and called me back.

"Come here," she said, with a hint of sadness in her voice. She wrapped her arms around me tightly and squeezed me. She knew I'd be fighting this time, too.

"Be careful Geoff, you know what he's like. Will you ring me when it's done?" She looked in to my eyes as she spoke, she knew it was going off, I admired her perception.

"Yea, alright, but If I get stabbed to death," I said with my very own kind of black humour and wagging my finger at her, "don't you kiss any other boys for at least a fortnight."

I laughed as she slapped my shoulder.

"Don't talk like that Geoff, you know I don't like it. You're sick."

I smiled and kissed her gently on the lips then walked to my car, half way down the path Sharon said with a tease in her voice,

"You know I'd wait at least three weeks."

"Cow," I laughed as I got in to the car and drove off.

Three days before, a friend and fellow doorman was killed by a single stab wound to the heart outside a Coventry nightclub in the city centre. When his convulsing frame fell to the pavement, five young men kicked his dying body again and again and again. He died on the way to hospital, so I understood why she was tense, she had every reason to be worried. 'Mr R' had glassed, stabbed, bottled, razored and petrol bombed many before me. He battered old, young, firm, infirm, able and disabled without hesitation or prejudice. A couple of months previously he had shoved a heavy, glass ashtray into the face of the amiable bar cellar man at the Lion, bludgeoning it into a gaping, bloody wound that needed a hundred stitches and a week in hospital to heal, and all for refusing to serve him with a drink. The dark side was definitely his soul mate.

On the five minute drive to the Lion, I sang to the tune of Elton John's 'Crocodile Rock', reverberating from the car stereo. My voice held the customary pre-fight shake that, over the years, I'd come to know well and hate, but it was all part of the build-up. I just ignored the feeling. To try and counter or fight it was futile and energy wasting. No, better to let it have the run of my body until the time came to release it in ferocious violence. The way to handle fear was to step right in to it and be a part of it.

The car park was relatively full, so I concluded that the Lion was busy. I parked my car at the front of the pub and walked in through the double red doors. There he was, directly in front of me, standing ten feet away at the bar with his 'Scotch' friend, drinking lager. The adrenaline shot through the spaghetti and filled my chest. I took a deep breath in.

As was usual in these situations, all eyes fell upon me and the space I was occupying. As I had surmised the room was full of drinkers. Two old, tortoise-faced men, still dressed in their Sixties Sunday best, sat crouched over glasses of slowly depleting beer in the nook to the left of the entrance door, talking about 'when I was a lad' and 'the kids today, they don't know they're born'. The beer pregnant regulars holding up the bar at the bend were slurring the world's problems to right. Young apprentice slobs knocked the balls around the pool table and bragged about the amount of beer they could drink, and dreamed of one day being 'real' regulars who could drink fifteen pints and still walk home.

"This belly's all paid for," they'd say, picking up their fat from the belt and juggling it like ten pounds of spuds. A pretty-faced little girl nicknamed 'five two' (so named because she bet one of the doormen a 'blow job' that she could beat him at pool, she lost five games to two and gave him a little 'head' in the car park - she had the kind of seductive look that made me think she may have lost on purpose, whenever she's in there's a huge queue at the pool table to play her) gave me a wink as I passed, no time for pool today. I took the measure of both men as I approached. Willmot Brown was nowhere to be seen.

'Mr R' looked very heavy set, wearing a grey, silky tracksuit and cheap, shiny trainers (I hate cheap, shiny trainers!). His fat arse sat in the pants of the fashion-starved silk bottoms like a bag of sprouts. His 'Scotch' companion was lighter in weight, though tall, and . . . Scottish. With his guttural, Glasgow accent he could have been eight stone and still sounded aggressive. His drink glazed eyes below a cap of blond hair, met mine on approach.

I went straight for 'Mr R' with the aggressive approach, but knew my heart wasn't in it, even before I started I knew he wasn't going to have any of it, knew I was the absolute cheekiest bastard in the world for even trying, but try I did. I don't like to employ physical tactics unless it's completely necessary.

Round the corner of the Lion car park John and Craig, the doormen who were supposed to be working tonight, were bent into the boot of Craig's Sierra. They were getting the 'bats'.

Craig was a tough ex-soldier, big at fourteen stone with large hunched shoulders that looked in a permanent state of 'mid shrug', and a face that looked in a permanent state of 'mid frown' with a thick square chin. His thinning blond hair was brushed forward to hide the 'thinning' bit. He grabbed the baseball bats from the car, passing one to Catalogue John, (he looked like a catalogue model) who stood hugely and handsomely at seventeen stone. The bat looked foreign in his hands like a barbie doll with an 'oozie'.

"Lets 'urry up, Geoff should be 'ere in a minute. Willmot said he's rang 'im up." (Lads, lads, I'm in there already.)

"Does he want us to wait for him, then?" said John, twirling the bat in his hands and nearly dropping it.

"Yea, 'e said to wait for 'im."

They walked, bats in hand, back around to the front door of the pub, unaware that I was already inside.

'Mr R' half turned as I approached, then turned back face toward the bar showing no respect and even less fear. I got straight to the point.

"You've got to leave!"

He turned and met my glance, he must have sensed the lack of commitment in my voice. His beetle, black-eyed, hard, empty stare went from me to the near full glass of beer that sat beside him like a faithful companion on the bar. He pointed to the said glass, letting me know that he'd got a pint and wasn't leaving. The 'dumb' tactic was an old trick, 'street speak' often used by people of his ilk, aimed at belittling you, not even showing you enough respect to speak, an attempt at psyching you out, but I'd been in this room before and knew all the tricks. His insolence only angered me. I shot again,

"You're barred, you've got to leave."

He looked at me again, and shook his head, his insolence was frightening because I knew it meant that he was ready to fight.

"It's a new gaffer, so I'm not barred." He slowly lifted the glass to his mouth and drank a gulp, then continued. "I'm not leaving."

Again he turned his back on me. The slur in his voice told me he'd had a few, the tone of his voice told me he wasn't buying my bluff, not today thank you.

"Listen, I'm telling ya', you've goda' leave."

"No!" he said, arrogantly. Again he pointed at his pint. (What was wrong with this man? Couldn't he say 'pint'?) I went for the kill, this would be my last attempt at a 'psych out'. My feet were already positioned in a small forty-five degree stance, ready for the possibility of 'physical'.

"If you don't leave now, we're gonna be fighting."

And why not, it had worked before, loads of times.

He eyed me suspiciously, looking for any signs of hesitance and fear in my voice. I felt the hesitance and the fear, so I guess it's fair to say that he spotted it too, but I didn't mind because it would feed his ego and sporn over-confidence. I also knew that the more fear I held, the better I would perform, providing I could hold onto it.

My mind stretched back in one second of silence between my challenge and his reply. I remembered the three hundred plus fights I'd won without defeat over the last eight years of working in this 'bastard' trade. I wondered in a millisecond of negativeness whether the law of averages was on my trail and if this would be my coup-de-grace. Could this be the one I lose? In fact, faced by two violent, big men, might I even die. Since my friend was stabbed and killed I'd thought a lot about life and death. He was a handy lad, a more than capable fighter and now he was dead. I thought about Sharon, who'd been asking me for a while now to start cutting out the door work, and my mum, who worried herself sick about me being involved in violence, even about Nina, my ex-wife, who begged me to leave the profession when we were married, and my kids. Was it all worth it?

I crushed the thoughts quickly, as a matter of urgency.

"Then we'll have to fight," he replied evenly.

'Fuck,' I never expected that. Scotch turned towards me, his back to the bar, ready to go. I made a mental note of his movement. 'Mr R' turned away from me in a fit of arrogance. I knew I had to hit him and I could sense that any second now he, or his mate, was going to strike out. Two years ago, my two bombastic friends would have both been unconscious by now, but at a mellow thirty-two and a third dan in Karate, I was trying desperately to transcend violence, to talk the talk, instead of walk the walk. With my fighting ability reaching maturity and my accuracy at its very best, I worried constantly about killing someone when perhaps I might have been able to 'talk it out'.

The danger was looming fast, the challenge had been thrown and accepted, there was nothing left to do but fight (or run). Every second that I delayed my pre-emptive attack would dig a deeper hole for me. I wasn't just facing one opponent I was facing two, and both had subliminally told me that they were prepared to 'go for it'. This was the hard part, the part where I knew I was going to get physical, the part where every negative part of my persona dared me to 'stay', where your legs start to shake and you feel weak, oh, so weak, and you think that your attack isn't going to work, and your arsehole feels like it's going to blow a gasket.

"So you're not going to go then?" I said, bringing my right hand back as though to say 'there's the door' and engaging his brain with a question to give my shot a blind second to land while his brain was tangled with thinking of an answer.

Craig and fucking Catalogue John were still waiting outside the front door for me to arrive, unaware that I was inside facing two of Jim Henson's puppet monsters. Willmot Brown was upstairs in the living quarters, looking out of the window for me to arrive (I'm here, I'm here), probably cursing me for taking so long. You'd think that one of the three would have noticed my car outside the front door? Craig and John were probably sitting on it waiting for me.

'BANG!' I pummelled my right fist into 'Mr R's' fat jaw line. I felt the heavy contact of knuckle on bone and knew it was a good one, his eyes closed and his face shuddered, he fell heavily sideways towards the beer-sodden tiled floor. The glass of beer he was holding left his hand and spun in the air, almost in slow motion, spewing beer in this direction and that. My right foot met his descending head before it hit the floor, taking his front teeth out. I kicked him so hard that it hurt my foot, blood splattered all over my lovely Fila trainers and socks. His faced splashed against the floor emitting a low hollow thud that made my stomach turn. As he lay motionless at my feet, beer and blood running in a river around his head and seeping in to his silver track suit top like an explosion transfer, I brought the heel of my right foot heavily down on his face and let out a blood-curdling 'KIAAA!' I hated doing this, but knew I had to, for survival. If this bastard gets up I could lose, and that frightened me.

'Scotch' jumped on my back to save his mate from any more punishment, so I threw him off and buried a left roundhouse into his belly, only slightly catching him as he scuttled out of the way. I chased him around the bar to no avail: I looked back at 'Mr R', he was beginning to stir.

'BANG!' Another kick that splattered into his already smashed face sent him back to sleep. 'Haggis' was on my back again like the proverbial haversack, again I threw him off and chased him away. He stopped at the bar, covering his unconscious mate from my punishing feet.

"What's your name?" The guttural, Glaswegian shouted, implying that he wanted to know the name so that, at a later date, he could 'get me sorted'.

"Geoff Thompson," I shouted back. "Ask anyone."

He didn't have to ask, he'd heard the name. I was the crazy bastard who roamed Woodend with a sword looking for a burglar not so long back. On hearing my name he tried to smash the plastic 'Carling Black Label' sign off the bar to use as a weapon against me, but he couldn't break it (he obviously didn't drink Carling Black Label) so he opted for the deadly weapon given to everyone who enters a public house, a beer glass. He promptly smashed it off the bar, splinters detonating in every direction like little glass spears. He pointed its jagged razor edges menacingly in my direction.

The crowds of people in the pub had long since fell deathly silent, the D.J. had stopped playing the music, a huge circle had formed to give us a fighting ground. 'Mr

R' lay, still unconscious, on the cold and unfriendly floor of defeat, blood seeping liberally from his face.

Gasps left many mouths as the glass shattered on the bar. What to do, what to do? I didn't like the look of the glass and certainly didn't want to be wearing it.

I coolly picked up a pint glass from one of the many abandoned tables and emptied its contents onto the carpet, then casually smashed my glass off the nearest table and walked towards my Scotch friend.

The look in his eyes said,

'Beam me up Scottie', and I guessed he'd only broken the glass as a defensive measure, but all the same, he had broken it. We faced off taking each other's measure.

'So,' I thought, 'it's a glass fight you want, is it?'

In the mayhem Willmot Brown had come down the stairs and witnessed the fight. He ran out of the front doors to look for Craig and John, wondering why they weren't in there already.

"CRAIG, JOHN! QUICK, INSIDE, GEOFF'S FIGHTING. QUICK. COME ON!"

'CRASH!' The double front doors of the pub burst open. Craig and John burst in wielding baseball bats.

I threw my glass on the floor.

They say you can smell fear, of course you can, especially when your opponent shits himself.

"PUT THE FUCKING GLASS DOWN!" I demanded. Scotch's eyes went from me to Craig, then from Craig to Catalogue John. "Put your glass down or you're gonna get battered," I told him. His eyes then fell onto the bats that the lads were wielding.

"Give me your word that my mate won't get any more," he said. (Brave bastard.)

I really admired his bottle, faced by three men, two carrying bats and he was prepared to get a battering to protect his mate. It would have been easy here to dish out some serious pain, but I respected this man's courage.

"You've got my word."

His eyes never left Craig and John as he extended his hand toward me (the one without the 'glass jewellery').

"Give me your hand," he said.

(But that'll only leave me with one.) I took the hand and shook it.

"You've got my word."

He immediately released his weapon.

"Nobody touch him," I shouted to the doormen. At this, myself and the now harmless 'Scotch', carried the still unconscious and now toothless 'Mr R' off the premises. Every voice in the whole room, that a moment ago seemed frozen in a muted second of time, chattered excitedly. The D.J. put on another record, civility was restored.

As 'Mr R's' heavy, blood sodden, toothless body fell onto the tarmac outside the pub, I told 'Scotch',

"When he comes around, tell him I'll meet him any time, any place if he wants to 'go' again."

Shortly afterwards, I was reliably informed that the pair battered a taxi driver who refused to 'taxi' them.

Willmot was over the moon, he slipped me a monkey for my troubles.

"There's no need Bill, I didn't do it for the money."

He winked and tucked the cash tightly in to my hand.

"Job done, job done, it's nice to be nice, as you do, as you do."

I laughed and took the money. Bill always made me laugh, he would take all the fashionable sayings around at the time like 'as you do' and string them into sentences that never meant anything: 'Job done, as you do'. I put my arm around him, gave him a hug and shook my head as I laughed,

"What are you like, Bill?"

This situation is still in the air (at the time of writing, 1993). 'Scotch' has sent down several messages apologising profusely for his behaviour. I admired him greatly for backing his mate on the night, he's a very brave man, I just can't understand what he's doing knocking around with a waster like 'Mr R'. 'Mr R' has sent down several messages saying he's going to shoot me. I, as a bit of insurance, obtained his home address, as I always do with people who cross swords with me, just in case!

A week later the threats are lessening and the stress aftermath has almost lost its impetus. Life is again returning to normal, though of course, I'm still on my guard. I'm always on my guard.

5. Money For Old Rope

Colin was an amiable enough chap of about twenty years old, five foot eight inches and thin, with long black, curly hair and a gaunt face. Not the most intelligent of people but not stupid either. He lived at home with this mum and step-dad and worked by day in a Rugby garage owned by P. When he wasn't working, he spent most of his time and money in the C public house on the Bolton Road, where he was a popular regular. Life was quite sweet until his boss at the garage gave him the sack for reasons unknown. In a small, one horse, town like Rugby, jobs were hard to come by, so Colin was understandably devastated.

One night, after an evening in the C, he decided to get revenge on his former boss by hitting him where it really hurt, in his Rolls Royce. Colin knew the car was his absolute pride and joy and that any damage he could do to the said vehicle would be as good as kicking the man straight in the bollocks, which he'd like to do as well, but never had the guts. His first tactical error was telling one or two of his buddies in the C (as you do when you've just drank seven pints of lager) of his intentions.

"Thinks 'e can just get rid of me and that's the end of it? 'E's got another thing coming."

Almost immediately after emptying a two pound bag of sugar into the petrol tank of the Roller, completely fucking up the engine, everyone in the sparsely populated neighbourhood, where even flatulence made the news headlines, knew who and why, and probably even where he bought the sugar.

This was by far his biggest mistake, a mistake that would alter the course of his whole life, drastically.

Six thousand pounds worth of repairs later, P was more than a little perturbed and absolutely had to, just had to have revenge. He didn't want to involve the police because all that meant was months of waiting for a court date and years of waiting for compensation from a judicial system that was slower than a lame tortoise. And then there was his credibility: how could he retain his image as a hard man/crook if he involved the police? He fancied himself as the toughest man in Rugby (which is a little like being the toughest man in your street). No, better to do it like they do in the films and put a contract out on Colin, that way he would get his revenge and not only retain his image but heighten it to the realms of gangster class. Yes, no one would fuck with him after that.

He knew a few doormen in neighbouring Coventry, where 'mad bastards' were in abundance. They'd sort it out for him. A phone call to L with the offer of £1000 for a good job done, and it was sorted.

"Of course I want the money for the repairs, L, but I also want you to teach this boy a lesson. He needs to know that I'm not a man to be messed with, you know what I'm saying, don't you?"

"Oh yea, P, it's not a problem, I'll get the lads to sort it."

L was a thick set, forty-eight year old with greying hair, a generous nose and a constant, irritating fidget like he was permanently waiting for a late bus. He ran a Coventry door agency and held many contacts.

A chain of phone calls was made. L rang M, a huge man with J.C.B. bucket hands and a face that'd scare your kids, who rang his brother-in-law S. He, in return, rang D. Together, and for a guaranteed £250 a piece, a good job was ensured. After all, they worked the door and gave out 'slaps' frequently anyway. £250 was just icing on the cake.

After a brief conversation and absolutely no planning the lads decided to go over to Rugby to check out the target and eye up the territory. M drove, S and D sat in the passenger seat and rear seat respectively. L stayed at home, his end of the deal was already completed. He was no mug, he was being paid for organising the job: you could do that on the phone, there was no need to take any risks.

D, from Willenhall, was the black sheep of his family and was well akin to violence, working on any door that would pay him and fighting with any man who dared cross him. Blond, handlebar moustache, under a pug nose with small light blue eyes below a hat of blond hair. Hugely built at seventeen stone, he looked like a cardboard cut-out of Hulk Hogan. S sat behind him, so big at six foot five inches, and nineteen stone, that he had to crouch his head under the roof of the Cortina. He had an infectious laugh and a sharp wit. A couple of neck bolts and S could have doubled for Herman Munster.

The car groaned under the combined weight of fifty-two stone as it chugged towards Rugby. Up the busy Binley Road, onto the Brandon Road, passing the tranquil Wolston and the beautiful, countrified Long Lawford, then into quiet Rugby to the popular C public house, which sat regally at the top of six steps: lounge to the left, bar to the right and a lovely garden to the rear. Understandably, many eyes glanced as they entered the plush lounge of the pub. Each of the three looked like heavies from a Sixties gangster movie. Colin was quickly spotted from a small photo M had been given. M, in his wisdom, decided to approach Colin and have a quiet word in his ear, D and S stood back so as not to look too ominous, indeed a difficult task.

There was a tenseness in the air that D and S knew well. It was neither welcomed nor shunned, it was just the expected introduction to violence. To the locals it was as welcome as a barbed, hedgehog shit and an unwelcome addition to their Sunday afternoon drinking session.

Unbeknown to D and S, M made a little deal with Colin.

"Colin," M tried to mimic affection, but that's not easy when you've got a voice with muscles, "you know the crack, you know why we're here, we're getting good money to break something but it doesn't have to be, we could sort it out."

Colin nodded in a capitulating manner, his mouth slightly ajar like a dumbstruck schoolboy.

"Can you sort out the money for the Roller by next week?"

"Er, Yea, I fink so." Of course he knew he couldn't but he wasn't going to tell that to these monsters.

M felt pleased with himself, for all his size and experience with violence he was basically a good man, if he could 'sort' this fellow without 'pain' he would. He patted Colin on the shoulder, his wan face flushing from blanket white to red.

"Good man, I'll tell you what to do. Hang a sling around your shoulder and we'll tell the man that we've done a job on ya', O.K.?"

Colin nodded affirmatively.

"Then give me a ring next week, when you've got P's money," M rubbed his thumb and forefinger together to underline 'money' "for the car repairs, and no one will be any the wiser." M gave him a knowing wink. "I'll even slip you a ton for your troubles."

This brought a smile to Colin's face. Both delighted with the deal, they parted company, Colin promised to get the money and M gave him a contact number to ring when he had.

In the car on the way back to Coventry the lads talked about what had been said in the pub. M never told them about his 'little deal'.

"So wot's the score?" asked D in a naturally gruff voice.

"Yea, wot d' 'ave to say for himself? Did you tell 'im wot 'e wus gonna get if he don't get the money?" added S.

"Don't worry, don't worry, he knows the score, I've given him to next Sunday to sort it. He's fucking shitting bowling balls, he's not gonna fuck."

"I 'ope 'e doesn't for 'is sake, weedy little bastud, 'e was a right streak of piss. If you 'ad 'ave spit on 'im 'e'd 'ave strangled."

S and D laughed.

"I can't see any of the locals getting involved if we do 'ave to sort 'im, they were a right load of country bumpkins, looked like they 'ad hay 'n' manure f' brains.

By the following Sunday Colin hadn't rung.

M contacted S and D, his plan hadn't worked.

"He's gonna have to have a slap," he told D on the phone. "Little wanker, I was really nice to 'im as well."

"How ya gonna work it then?"

"We'll give him a little bit of a slap, then give him another couple of days to get the money together, we'll have to give him some pain, though, or he won't take it serious."

"Who's gonna do it, me 'n' S?"

"Yea, I think so, I'll drive the car. It won't take much whoever does it. You'd have more trouble fighting the current when you pull the plug after having a bath."

"I'll bring some thin' wi' me, just in case."

M rang L.

"What do you think, do you want us to give 'im some?" Even over the phone M could sense L fidgeting around like a tramp's vest.

"Oh yea, he'll have to have it, that's what the man says. I don't think he ever really expects to see the money, he just wants to make an example."

Between them they decided to do it straight away, to get it over and done with.

That night, Sunday at eight p.m., for the second time they drove through the sleepy countryside that lay between

Coventry and Rugby to do the dirty deed, D armed with a twelve inch long piece of lead filled conjuit pipe.

The warm evening sun beat down on the slightly battered blue, 'S' reg. Cortina. D and S, who were, to be honest, pissed, laughed and joked all the way to the C. They thought little of the task that lay ahead, only that a cheeky, young, local lad was going to get a slap, nothing more than that, and they would all be £250 heavier in the hip pocket for it. None thought about the seriousness of the matter, nor the dire consequences that could, would follow. None thought either that, should they get caught, they could lose their homes, jobs, families, everything, and for what? £250.

They all just thought it was a bit of a wheeze. If they did get caught they'd only get a slap on the wrist, at the very most.

D and S stretched their taught, cramped muscles as they emerged from the car. M stayed in the driver's seat as getaway man.

Once out of the car and stretched, D's and S's moods changed. They got themselves in to fight mode, the genial, joking, clowning pair that travelled from Coventry transposed themselves into 'heavies'. They looked mean and ugly.

"I'll do it, you watch my back, alright?" D was very matter of fact, S nodded his assent.

"I'm not gonna fuck around, just in, give it 'im and away, anyone gets in my way you 'fuck' them."

S nodded again. The time for talk was over, they pounded into the pub.

The July sun shone the C public house into the frame of a picturesque country pub where gossiping banter quizzed across table tops, Lassie dogs sat obediently at their masters' feet and a portly, red-faced landlord stood sentry-like at the end of the bar drinking away profits and heading for a heart attack, leaving his spot very occasionally, and only then to pinch the barmaid's ample bottom. Local farmers with a taste for beer and a distaste for strangers sat at pine tables 'I'ing and 'R'ing in true yokel style and talking about how they 'carn't read and carn't wruyght, but they cun druyve a track-urr'. Would-be dart pro's with 'Jockey Wilson' bellies and plastic flighted darts hitting the board in all the wrong places were dreaming of one day playing the circuit. A fat lady with 'wide load' knickers underneath a navy crimplene dress that could tent a dozen boy scouts laughed hysterically and solemnly told her companions that she 'hardly eats a thing' and 'everything I do eat just turns to fat'.

Colin, ill-dressed like a field scare crow in Worzel Gummage hand-me-downs, sat quietly with his brother-in-law at a table close to the bar, sipping his usual half because 'I can't really afford to drink now that I haven't got a job', unaware of how close the mantle of retribution lay, and that he wouldn't be enjoying his half for much longer.

The lads entered the busy bar, D with the conjuit pipe tucked into his grey leather jacket. He felt good now, so did S.

Again all eyes were on them as they entered but this just blew their egos even larger. Colin was sat at a table with his father-in-law, a big, barrel-chested man of about forty with thinning hair, and a red, veined face that looked like a map of Europe. His eyes held a bloodshot hue. S approached the hapless Colin through the crowd of people, D followed, stopping a short distance back.

Smoke herded the air, the smell of country (shit) wafted in warm waves, whispers broke out in the room like a conspiracy, a hundred voices fusing into one inaudible hum. All eyes universally followed the two 'strangers': they stood out like eunuchs on a nudist beach.

D and S both breathed in deeply to control the flow, they were in mode, the fight was on.

"Can I have a little word with you outside?" S asked evenly.

Colin, who must have thought 'a word' really did mean 'a word' and not a battering, agreed effusively, but as he stood up to leave his brother-in-law grabbed him by the arm and pulled him back.

"He's going nowhere," he said staring at S and D defiantly. "Anything you've got to say to 'im can be said 'ere."

Colin's eyes went pathetically from the lads to his brother-in-law, and then back again, almost apologetically. For a moment there was a deathly silence, the room muted in anticipation. This was a complication that S and D hadn't counted for. Actually, they hadn't counted for anything other than a compliant victim.

D and the brother-in-law eyed each other like latter day gun fighters, the tension was palpable, the locals held their breath (this was more exiting than 'Emmerdale Farm').

D slowly pulled the lead pipe from his jacket.

"Is that right?" he asked, menacingly.

M, outside in the getaway car, was starting to get a little restless. He stood out here like a bulldog's bollocks: he was starting to regret the whole issue, it felt wrong, they'd not planned a single thing, save the fact that D was going to bash Colin with the pipe. No strategies, no false number plates or better still a stolen car, no alibis should it all go wrong, nothing. As he sat there in the car he realised what a balls up this could all be if complications should arise. They'd only been in there a couple of minutes but it seemed like an hour. Everyone that walked past the car looked in at him, he looked like he was on a 'hit'. 'Where the fuck are they?' he whispered to himself.

'BANG!' D put the pipe straight across the crown of Colin's head, bursting his skull into a gaping crimson vein of blood, his body spiralled and he fell face first, heavy and lifeless onto and through a table full of drinks, into the oblivion of unconsciousness.

For a split second no one moved as though frozen in time, then as one the whole pub exploded, the brother-in-law lunged angrily at D, only to be coshed just as quickly, and just as savagely. He crashed to the floor at D's feet, just holding onto his consciousness and grabbing hold of D's legs in a frantic attempt at keeping him in the pub, and in the hope that it may curb the 'caning' he was about to get.

As D battered him with the pipe again and again, a huge virago of a woman, who must have topped the scales at at least twenty stone, jumped on S's back, biting, scratching and pinching him. D was still whacking the brother-in-law, so much so that he lost control of the pipe and it disappeared under dozens of feet. As he smashed the brother-in-law's face through the glass patio doors in a last ditch attempt at releasing the leech, more attacking bodies flailed in at him, so he counter lashed in every direction: if it moved D hit it. As S spun around trying to get the 'fat piece' off his back, her chubby face came into D's view for a millisecond, so he punched her hard in the eye. She squealed and held the eye in an attempt at assuaging the pain, giving S a chance of breaking free (she shouldn't have been 'hanging' around strange men anyway). Together D and S fought their way through the doors and back onto the street and ran for the cramped sanctuary of the waiting Cortina.

M started the engine up ready to go. Before the lads reached the car D stopped dead in his tracks.

"Oh fuck!" he screamed.

"What?" shouted S.

"I've left the fucking conjuit pipe in the pub, it'll have my 'prints' all over it. We'll have to go back in."

S closed his eyes and shook his head in disgust.

'You stupid bastard, how could you do this to me?'

Without demur D and S ran back into the pub to retrieve 'the evidence'. As soon as the locals saw the pair the battle started again: punches, kicks, bites, butts and spits filled the screen as D and S fought their way back to get the pipe.

Amazingly, D found it, forlorn in a corner of the room by the smashed blood-stained patio doors. Quickly, amidst much violence, mayhem, smashed glass, spilt beer, toppled tables, shouts, screams, grunts and groans, they ran kicking, punching and 'piping' back through the crowds and out to the waiting car, where an impatient M whisked them off to comparatively quiet Coventry. All the way home, S and D laughed till their eyes smarted with tears and their stomachs cramped with effort. Their laughter was to be short lived.

The C public house had never seen such devastation and, although all had risen admirably and stoically to the occasion, they were now suffused with a cocktail of feelings, anger, fear, depression and confusion, fear swimming well clear of the maelstrom. Their lives were upside down in an instant, all of a sudden that overdue phone bill, leaking roof or marital argument seemed frugal by comparison.

This kind of violence was way beyond the purlieus of their mental capacity. Every blow, scream, spill of blood and smash of glass would be etched into their memories for ever more, bringing serenity closer to some, heart attacks and ulcers closer to others. Rising to violence on the spur and fighting without the common sense of thought as an interfering factor is very easy because it is instinctive, going way back to primeval days where mankind had to fight to survive and violence was as natural as eating and drinking. The aftermath of fear and stress, though, are not so easy to control or rise to making people's lives a misery.

Pedantic yet happy life in the C had changed immeasurably in an instant, mayhem had reared its ugly head and roared into their lives like an autumn gale.

Colin still lay motionless amidst a disarray of broken glass, spilled beer and upturned tables, deep in the wings of unconsciousness. His already pale hue paler for it, blood debauching itself liberally from the hideous crimson gash to his crown, seeping into and matting his hair. The fat lady, taking up three chairs and a small table (this thing won't be over until she sings) cried uncontrollably and nursed her swelling black eye, that looked comically absurd on such an obese face like a 'cartoon shiner'.

The brother-in-law, with a face of bloody melancholy, was holding a handkerchief to his head to stem the blood, his whole body rippling with an embarrassing, involuntary tremor.

"Bastards," was all he could muster every few seconds.

Many surrounded each victim, praising and sympathising in an attempt at mollifying their sorrow and pain. A fetid smell wafted around the room: Colin's bowels had emptied themselves, a large, dark, wet stain spreading around the crotch of his navy, cotton trousers like ink on blotting paper.

Colin's breathing was shallow and erratic, he looked on the verge of death. The ambulance was on its way.

To D and S, primeval fighting was a common occurrence. Most weekends would see them in the thick of battle in one pub or another. They grew to expect it, even like it. Both knew it was wrong but neither could or for that matter would pull themselves away from it. They both loved to walk into a pub and be instantly recognised as 'bouncers', fighters or 'fucking nutcases'. Liked never having to pay or queue into any pub or nightclub, and being the centre of attraction at work where even the foreman gave them a wide berth. Having plenty of women around them because of who and what they were. They knew that the violence and fighting was wrong, but the by-products made it more than worth their while.

The thought of being ordinary people frightened them, they liked being 'somebody'. In their own environment they were stars. Their girlfriends loved it too (though they would never admit to it), always telling the lads to get off the door and stop fighting but never complaining when they got VIP treatment off the doormen and managers in the nightclubs and pubs, often being fed for nothing in the Indian restaurants, or if they were out with the girls, being pulled, in front of waiting queue of people, to the front of the line and ushered in for free. Bouncing, D had surmised, might well be a mug's game, but he was the best dressed, best treated, most respected mug he'd ever known.

D had a good steady job in the day, at the Jaguar car plant, moving bits and pieces around all day on the fork-lift truck. 'The Door', though, was beginning to envelope him, taking over his life. He'd started doing the odd night here and there for a bit of pocket money, not realising it would suck him in like a whirlpool and not let him go. Before he knew it, he was working every night and in charge of several teams, and answering only to L, who paid him handsomely for his trouble. D had the look of a fighter and the absolute respect of his men, his soft side betrayed occasionally by the twitch in his small blue eyes, that for a fleeting second, made him look cute and vulnerable. He enjoyed his work so much that he was seriously thinking about giving up his day job for it. Many before him had done so and regretted it.

The life of a doorman is, or can be, short lived. After a few years of it, maybe even a few months, when the novelty wears off, he'll be praying for a straight job, praying for a life without violence and its ugly handmaiden, stress, praying for a quiet night at home with the wife and kids, praying for a life. Freedom from strife is precious, a gift from God. But, alas, sometimes you have to be starved of it before you realise its real worth and importance.

When the phone rang in the front room of D's smart, well furnished, Binley house, D picked it up without demur. Later when stress and fear got a claw-like grip on him, he'd learn to hate the ring of the phone, its ring becoming synonymous with bad news and trouble. It was Thursday night, six-thirty p.m., almost time for his last night shift of that week.

"D," said the nervous, shaky, disembodied voice on the other end of the line. It was S's sister who was married to M, the getaway driver. "The police have been around looking for M."

D didn't answer, his whole body flooded with a lorry load of fear-peppered adrenaline. He felt his bowels twitch uncomfortably and his mind buzz with a paroxysm of thoughts, questions and analyses, all fighting for the front and demanding answers to the questions they posed. Sun Tzu said that those who wish to 'wage war' should first count the cost.

Aftermath had arrived. The second fight, the real fight, had just begun.

M and S worked together in the family business, 'Neat Sheet Metal Co.' (for want of a better alias). M was oblivious at that time to the police visit. He was happy and content, last weekend was already lost in his memory where it lay sleeping like a slumbering, fireside dog. It was just another 'situation'. They hadn't been paid for it yet, either.

The small factory unit lay neatly in a family of units, recently built on the clean industrial estate that lay precariously between Potters Green, cosy Aldermans Green and Woodend like a piece of prime ham between two pieces of soft, fresh bread with half a dozen ants crawling all over it. When M saw the police car pull slowly into his works car park, he felt all the same feelings that D had done, only worse. After all, it was his phone number that 'unconscious Colin' was holding, something he'd neglected to tell the lads and something he hoped, nay prayed would not come to light, though deep down he knew it eventually would. He quickly ran into the small office of the factory to S,

"Quick, fuck off out the back, the law's here." He shooed him urgently with his hands as he spoke.

When S saw the panda car out of the office window he disappeared out of the factory, and made his way straight down to the pub. A couple of pints would definitely, he assured himself, help to put things a little into perspective. If not, a few more would help put him into an uncaring, comatose, burping, farting heap.

M was taken straight to the station for questioning (do not pass Go, do not collect two hundred pounds).

At the other end of the city, D sat alone with loneliness in a rough Willenhall bar where the locals picked their teeth with Katanas, and shot guns were as perfunctory as the tables and chairs. He was comfortable here, these were his kind of people, rough as sod but straight. He was searching for what S had already found . . . oblivion.

Within an hour of the police arresting M, they were on D and S's tracks. Even before they had picked any of the lads up they knew everything, there was so many witnesses that the case was already watertight. Still, it wouldn't hurt to get confessions as well. M had vowed not to open his mouth, promised for his and the lads sakes to say nothing. He could handle it, he knew he could.

As soon as the C.I.D. got him alone, they knew they could trick him. They'd seen it all, people who were tough and people who only thought they were, those who knew the crack, and others who never had a fucking clue. M was tough, but he hadn't any idea about police procedure, the games they play and the little white lies they tell to get you to talk (he obviously doesn't watch 'The Bill'.)

The D.C. in charge, a hard eyed, gum chewing, smart, soldier-like character, with an air of arrogance that came with his badge at Ryton (police training school) couldn't believe his luck. Every trick he tried on M had worked, starting straight away with the,

'You do realise the seriousness of this charge, don't you?' ploy, which shook M right from his boots. After telling M how much trouble he was in and that he could be looking at a charge of attempted murder, and 'you might as well own up because we know everything anyway', they left him in a bare room with only a table and chair for his mind to play with for nearly an hour. They knew that his own mind would do most of the work for them, spiralling him down into ever increasing misery until he would desperately snatch at any offer they made him.

After an hour, M was, to say the least, perturbed but still holding on. He'd managed to deny everything until D.C. Bustard pulled out his ace card, shooting M down in absolute and utter flames.

"I'm telling you now that if you don't start getting a little more co-operative," he emphasised the word 'co-operative', "you're gonna have the whole fucking lot. We don't really give a monkey's fuck whether we get the others or not, as long as we've got you. Think about it, you're already looking at attempted murder, if you don't tell us your part in it we're gonna add blackmail and extortion."

M's eyes shot forward in surprise.

"You're gonna be looking at some serious time."

He'd got M on the run. He paused deliberately to let the seriousness of the words sink in, then continued.

"Look at the fucking size of you, man. What jury in the world is going to believe it wasn't you? You could be a fucking priest looking like that and they'd still send you down the steps. Do yourself a big favour and give us what we want, it'll save a lot of fucking around in the long run."

The words sliced him to pieces, cut his will to the bone, crushed it flatter than paper. Could they really do that? Was it possible? He guessed so or they wouldn't have said it. And if he went down, what would become of the lady he adored and lived every waking hour for and the beautiful children (they become more beautiful when you think you're going to lose them) they had reared together and who doted on him. What would become of them? Life wouldn't be without his family. Perhaps the police were bluffing, but he couldn't take the chance. What about the lads though, he couldn't give them up, but if he didn't his family would be taken away from him. The D.C. threw a pile of witness statements on the table in front of him.

"We've got you anyway, M, it'll make it easier on you and the lads if you give us a full confession."

He thought for a long moment, shook his head in a hope that perhaps it was all a bad dream. His face held a look of defeat. A short time later S was arrested at home. D, on hearing of the two arrests, went on another mad drinking spree instead of going to work that night. After all, if he was caught and remanded in custody, who knows when he might get another chance?

D's blonde, slim wife lay, head on his chest, in the darkened bedroom of their house, twelve-thirty a.m. and they still weren't asleep.

"What's going to happen, D, will it mean prison?"

D was quiet for a moment.

"Naw," he tried to console her, "we'll get of with a warnin'. No one ever gets bird first time around, anyway there's hardly any room in the jails so they're giving out loads of community hours. You just look sad in the courts, tell 'im you're sorry and 'e'll give ya loads of old ladies' gardens to dig."

He said it, but he didn't believe it, neither did she.

That night, despite having a good drink in him, D tossed and turned, not even finding a sanctuary in his own bed. There's no hiding place from stress, you have to just stand and fight . . . or fall. D's lovely wife was probably the only person in D's world who knew the real man, the soft, sensitive side to this hugely muscular man of violence. She shared his sleeplessness. He was a bit of a rogue, she knew, but she loved the very ground he walked on and wondered how she'd cope if he had to go to prison.

D spent the next couple of days slipping the rapidly closing police net. Through the grapevine, he was told,

"Give yourself up, or it'll be worse for you when we do get you."

Bowing to the inevitable, D did give himself up. As the panda drove D over to Rugby Police Station he felt relief that it was over and he'd been 'nabbed'.

"You do realise," said D.C. Bustard, relishing in D's plight, "that you could be charged with attempted murder."

This part truth, part ploy left D's temporary relief in a sorry state of decimation. As his face flushed red, his bottom spewed out a blast of wind that choked the car like C.S. gas. Even the noxious smell of D's unloaded anal passage didn't, though, wipe the smile off the face of D.C. Bustard, who'd never enjoyed so much success. He mentally rubbed his hands together with glee.

Initially, S and D, both knowing the crack, denied everything and pleaded not guilty to all charges, until they were shown the overwhelming evidence against them. M's statement, the phone number off Colin, witness statements from the C public house, and a witness who saw the three hurriedly getting into the car outside the pub and jotted down the number plate.

The game was up.

D admitted his part in it and was charged with a Section 18 wounding with intent, eventually getting it dropped to the lesser, though still serious, Section 20 wounding.

S still denied his part in it all, despite everything else. This denial was agitating the police no end. After all, everyone else was playing the game, so why shouldn't S? He needed a little friendly persuasion. D.C. Bustard was pretty good at 'friendly persuasion'.

"Plead to Section 20," he told S, "or we're going to charge you with attempted murder, blackmail and demanding money with menaces." (Get your head round that bastard.)

By comparison, S thought Section 20 looked pretty damned good, so snapped the D.C.'s hand off.

By January of the next year, the lads had been to court six times, each time with adjournment due to social reports, etc. Late January saw them in Crown Court under the judgeship of one of the county's most formidable judges, famous around these parts for his harsh sentences and hatred for the criminally penurious. Obviously they were guilty before they even started on account of the fact that they'd pleaded guilty, it was just a case of sentencing. S, D and M, (L & P never got roped in), were all pretty sure that they would get away with a severe reprimand, commonly known as a slapped wrist. The judge didn't see it quite like that. In summing up at the end of the trial, he said,

"This is the worst case of unprovoked violence I've ever witnessed, relating back to the blackmailing, racketeering gangsters of the Sixties. I shall very reluctantly grant you bail whilst we await social reports, but I warn you now, prepare yourselves for custodial sentences."

3rd March 1989 - the lads stood, dressed in their best 'court suits' in the dock to await sentence. They all still hoped to escape a jail term, but realistically they knew that they never had a 'frog on road's chance'.

Their sentences were announced: S, thirty months in prison. D, thirty months in prison. M, thirty months in prison.

S thanked the judge effusively. D and M bowed their head low as they were all led 'down the steps'.

"Brilliant, great," said a rejoicing S as they were led to a cell underneath the courts. "We'll be out in six weeks."

D lifted his burdensome head up, and looked at S, bemused.

"Six weeks? 'Ow the fuck do you make that out?"

"Well," began S, smiling broadly "three months sentence, with good behaviour, we'll be out in six weeks."

D shook his head, disbelievingly.

"Thirty months, you stupid cunt, not three months."

S's lower lip hit the floor in disbelief and his legs wobbled. He felt faint. D was a 'buttock tensing' millisecond away from soiling his undergarments and his head was 'out there with Pluto'. M's whole body shook, he thought he'd died and gone to hell.

In the cell awaiting transport to Winston Green, they sang,

"We're all going on a summer holiday."

Thirty months was the prison sentence they received. D also lost his job, his car, his liberty and two precious years out of his children's lives.

M lost his business, his credibility, his dignity, his liberty and also two years out of his children's lives.

S lost his business, his flat, his car and his liberty.

'Unconscious Colin' never recovered fully from his head wound and now walks around in a drunken stupor, slurring his words and seemingly oblivious to all and sundry. He'll never work again.

All this, and no money ever changed hands.

6. 'Pigs' In The Middle

Pretty girls at an 'acid party' are always in abundance, and on this warm July night it was altogether too much for me and my little mate 'downstairs' (my willy). To take my mind off the frustrating arousal and the terrible din these people called music, I let my mind wander back three hours to Nobby's Place where I sat with a half of lager waiting for my lift. They were late. They said they'd be here by midnight but it was twelve-thirty a.m. I wanted to go home, oh God, I wanted to go home, but the £100 I was promised for working the Hinckley acid do was too much to turn down. All the same if they didn't come for me soon I was going home. A warm bed seemed more attractive right now than a ton in the bank. The headlights of the red Nissan Bluebird estate flashed three times through the back entrance window of Nobby's. A lead weight pulled down at my heart and I heaved a heavy, tired, pissed off sigh.

'Oh shit'. The bubble of a warm bed burst and I was on my way. We left the city centre and before my sleepy eyes knew it we were on the M69 towards Leicester.

The car was filled with a mixture of doormen and punters. Gaz, a short, stocky, moustached friend of mine, drove. Everyone in the car was talking but it all sounded garbled because I was too tired to be interested. I lifted my bottom off the seat to release my sweat-sticky trousers from my legs. A black guy next to me with half closed eyes lit up a spliff and drew heavily upon it, held the smoke in his mouth momentarily then billowed it out like furnace fumes, filling the car. This brought a whole new meaning to the words 'passive smoking'. I felt my frowning mouth lift involuntarily into a grin and as my eyes widened my heart began to jump and dance under my shirt. I instinctively breathed in deeply through my nose and my fingers tapped my legs merrily to the beat of the music that a moment ago didn't seem to exist.

'Yes, yes, yes,' I thought, 'I can't wait to get there'.

The house was big, but just a dot in the middle of the fellowship of fields that surrounded it. The nearest neighbour was at least a mile away. The country lane the house sat in was wide enough for only one vehicle at a time. Cars were parked as far as the eye could see on the grass and in the ditches all the way down it. This huge, white, vacant house with high tiled roof boasted half an acre as its garden, every inch of which was covered by bopping, bouncing bodies. From the sky it must have looked like an army of ants around a sugar lump.

The monotonous, meaningless, lyricless music attacked my ears with merciless malice and I wondered if this was purgatory (yes, I didn't like the music).

Ten of us were guarding, six with Alsatian dogs. The eleventh was given his marching orders because his dog bit Tony 'the head' on the ankle with absolutely no provocation. Four of us were veteran doormen; the dog handlers, though, were just your run of the mill security. They would have served only as cannon fodder if it 'kicked of'.

I watched as two beautiful ladies paid entrance to the party, one tall with mousy brown hair, big eyes, lovely pouting lips and a body that would have awoken the beast in a priest. Her little high vest bared her mid-rift tantalisingly down to her black trousers that hugged her bottom tightly at the top before splaying out into bagginess at the leg. Her mate was blonde and just as pretty, slightly shorter but still tall. Her blouse was ghostly in its transparentness and I wondered if she really needed to wear it for what it covered? Her short skirt was figure-hugging and quite honestly, at first glance, I thought it was a belt. They walked onto the grass dance floor with a confidence that betrayed them for the policewomen they were.

Myself, personally, I'm very pro-police. I think they do a hard and thankless job, but my views were shared by none of the clientele at this rave. It was a mugger's mall, a crook's convention and a fighter's feast. There were some heavy, heavy people around who did not like the intrusion of the law, even if 'it' was off duty. They stood out like a bloody nose at a baptism and were as welcome here as Scabies.

When you've dealt with the law or have been dealt with by the law, you learn to sense it, smell it, even taste it. These two beautiful girls who had, quite honestly, only come out here for a good time. The arm of the law may well be long, but it wouldn't stretch to the aid of these two tonight. They were spotted instantly.

I watched with dismay as a ring of taunting youths encircled them. I eyed their faces as the beauty faded to pale. The organisers of the rave, who were also, as coincidence would have it, the leaders of the infamous 'Bell Green Crew', broke the circle and approached the girls menacingly.

"Wot's the crack? Wot the fuck are ya doin' 'ere? Spying, ya fucking spying are ya? You're law, I can smell you from 'ere."

The man with the questions was tall and ginger with a rugged face and twisted mouth. He had hate in his eyes and loathing in his tone.

The girls were frightened, non-plussed. They were only out for a good night, the last thing they wanted was trouble, especially in the middle of nowhere.

"No," said the blonde, we're just out for a good night, that's all."

"You're filth though, ain't ya?"

The dark haired girl spoke up.

"We are in the police, but that's not why we're here, we just thought . . ."

Ginger interrupted,

"Ya never thought fucking nothin', we don't want you 'ere, you're scum."

The blonde went for the obvious.

"Let us go then, we don't want any trouble, just let us go home."

"Oh yea, so you can ring your mates to come and close us down? You can stay 'ere for the rest of the night, where we can keep an eye on you."

The girls looked at each other in dismay.

For the rest of the night this was to be their prison. They couldn't leave until the next day and not then until the very last person had left. All the security were told that if they tried to leave they were to be hurt. If they let them go now they would surely inform their colleagues of the whereabouts of this illegal rave.

"Let's just batter them and fuck them out into a field," came one of the many suggestions. Many other threats and insults were maliciously tossed at the girls. I still watched from a short distance away. The taller of the two looked like a little frightened rabbit, the other didn't look too happy either.

Nev, the leader, stood tall, lean and meticulously smart from his £100 Torsion trainers through his Pepe jeans to his Tacchini top, even to the short side-parted soldier smart cut of his hair. His nose had a central break in it from one of his many pro-boxing bouts, but it only served to fine tune his character. Big in fashion he may have been, big in heart he definitely wasn't. Expressionlessly he listened to the girls pleading for their freedom. Their promise of secrecy hit a wall of heartlessness,

"Just let us go, we promise that we won't say anything, honest."

"No!" Nev underlined. "You stay here all night, it's as much as I can do to stop these people fucking you up, now keep out of my face."

I speculated that they might cry, and if they thought it would have helped I think they would have done, but it wouldn't, so they didn't.

The sound of a taxi pulling up outside the gates of the house distracted me. More party goers hitting for a high, slithered out of the black cab doors laughing and joking and completely unperturbed by the £25 entrance fee. Spotlights above the rave entrance shadowed the guards and their dogs and reflected off the roof of the purring cab.

I approached it, pushing my way through the hundreds of revellers, young and old, mostly young, walking through the guard. I poked my head through the side window of the taxi, (the driver thought this amusing because he hadn't wound the window down).

"Hang on a minute," I said to the flat-capped cabbie, "I've got someone to go back." He nodded his appreciation, another thirty quid. I walked back through the guards, through the punters, through the music and through the mayhem and stood in front of the girls in blue. They stared at me in unison looking deep into my eyes desperately seeking a friend. I held both my hands out towards them offering a lifeline. They took a hand each, everybody stared and whispered and pointed as I turned and walked hand in hand with these two beautiful, frightened ladies, back through the mayhem, the music, the punters, then the guards who looked at each other in astonishment. I felt good as they released their tight grip of my hands to get in the taxi.

The taxi was surrounded by revellers so it couldn't move off straight away. The girls looked scared. A panda car pulled up and Nev walked over to talk to them. The girls watched out of the taxi window and the moment was tense: I thought that they might call out to the police in the panda, but they did the exact opposite, they slid down on the seats and tried to hide. It was obvious that they didn't want to be seen. After a long minute the panda drove off, followed shortly after by the cab.

There was not a word spoken but the thanks was in their eyes as the taxi whisked them away.

I walked back through the guards, no one approached me, nobody spoke. This was respect.

7. Main En Main

To my mind, the ultimate act of courage is to fight one to one, or 'main en main', as the French might say. Why? Because to fight alone takes ultimate courage and self control. The only firepower you carry is that which lies within you. It doesn't matter who you know, who your 'back up' is or even how many Dans (black belt grades) you hold, because none of it counts when a 'straightener' is arranged. All your allies just step back and leave you to it and if you haven't got it the 'belt' will do nothing more than hold up your trousers.

'One on ones' always sort the men out from the boys, because eighty per cent of fighters (or so called) won't, or at least their bottle won't, stretch further than the purlieus of gang fighting where they are lost in the maelstrom of other fighters, and single minded courage isn't needed or called upon so much as in the 'one on one'. To stand alone with only the crutch of your own courage is the ultimate expression of bravery. I've seen fewer braver, and even fewer I admire more than a fellow schoolboy, many years ago at Cardinal Wiseman Boys' school, which held lessons for hundreds of working class boys around the city.

Every class in every school has its 'swats' and Wiseman was no exception. The 'swat' was the kid that never worked less than full out in class, was never naughty, never got dirty, and nearly always, without exception, wore round, bottle-bottomed glasses and never ventured out of the house without their sturdy steeds, the Parker pen and brown leather briefcase. Yes, as you can see, life for the 'swat' was a pen of excitement. Chewed topped Biro's and canvas rucksacks were absolute and utter sacrilege.

I, as a child, was a strange concoction that sat precariously on the fence between the two, never quite making up my mind which side of the enclosure I wanted to be on, longing to be one of the 'boys' with Doctor Martin boots, stay press trousers and cool barathea jacket that hung from my skinny frame like a Big Daddy overcoat, but enjoying the great rapport I held with the 'swats'. My babyface and dead giveaway briefcase, clashing terribly with the 'hard man' clothing, gave me the look of the proverbial fashion schizophrenic. In my latter years at school, when my own bullies and antagonists were tossed by the wayside and courage was born from it, I became the protector, dare I say crusader, of the 'swats', fighting off the 'boys' who always preyed upon them for being 'different' and not smoking and swearing in the darkest crevices and corners of the tarmac'd school playground. I walked then, as I do now, the fine and dangerous line between the literary and the criminally educated, gaining respect, I hope, from both quarters.

Dennis was definitely educated, but only in the world of the criminal, majoring in bullying where he was top of the class. He considered the 'swats' as subordinates whose staid gait infuriated him. Every day would see 'Dennis the menace' sweeping the playground like a tide of misery, taking money, sweets, pens, pencils and anything else that took his fancy from those weaker than himself, squashing those that argued back like newspapered bluebottles. Built like a pitbull, only more aggressive and less intelligent, Dennis was always fighting whether it was on the rugger field where even the referee gave him a wide berth, or in the boxing ring where they nicknamed him 'animal' because he simply was, or on the dance floor at the local disco where he ruled the roost. His rep as a fighter was as big as Elephant haemorrhoids (and that's pretty big). He cared not, either, that he drove misery into the hearts of everyone he crossed, like a sword. He knew that was his strength and he thrived upon it.

David was a 'swat' and sat quite neatly into the category that I have formerly described. Gold rimmed spectacles sat on a small, lily-white nose that was peppered with freckles, face pinched with fatigue, uniform meticulously clean down to the spit, polished shine on his shoes and neat mousy-coloured, side-parted hair. He was a prime target. He had 'victim' written all over him. Dennis had noticed him on more than one occasion; he was just waiting for the right moment.

After lunch-break one Wednesday afternoon Dennis pulled him. He was sure he could extort money or dinner tickets from this likely looking candidate, who looked like a mannequin in a school uniform shop.

A hundred kids of every ilk were crossing the pair, going to class in one of the two school blocks they stood between. Single storey Science block to the left, two storey English block to the right. Dennis poked David hard in the chest.

"Give me your money," he demanded menacingly. David, surprisingly, looked unperturbed.

I was one of the hundreds of kids crossing on my way to the English block. I stood a safe distance away and watched as David placed his brown leather briefcase on the ground beside him.

"No," he said without even a hint of fear in his voice, only despise. Dennis looked around him, not believing his own ears. He pushed David.

"What do you mean, no?" he challenged.

"How many different connotations does the word hold? No means no, no matter how you say it," David replied, belittlingly.

Dennis, who was to say the least, dumbfounded, had no conception of verbal arguments, so went for the familiar,

"If you don't give me your money, then we'll have to fight." 'That'll stop him in his tracks,' he thought.

"Alright," came David's calm and seemingly fearless reply.

Dennis's mouth gaped open in shock. This was a level he'd never had to rise to before. He felt a fear in his belly to which he wasn't akin and he didn't like it, and what the fuck does 'connotation' mean? Dennis looked around him at all the people milling to and fro and desperately searched for the sanctuary of a friendly face. This school didn't hold one for him. He laughed aloud and over-dramatically to try to hide his bafflement, then said, almost shouted, to no one in particular,

"He wants to fight me. He said he's not scared of anyone." He then looked back at David, whose eyes held a strength that unnerved him, frightened him. He felt out of his league, as though he didn't want to be there. In a bid to escape, Dennis tried to switch the onus from himself.

"So you'll fight anyone will you?" David knew this game, so put the onus straight back to Dennis.

"Yes anyone, but especially you. I'm not afraid of you."

Dennis's will was slayed. Another fake laugh left his lips, then he let himself get carried away in the tide of people.

"I'll see you again," Dennis threatened, unconvincingly. Then he disappeared on a sea of school kids into the Science block. David didn't even celebrate with a smile, just picked up his briefcase and walked, past me, to his lesson, not knowing how much I admired him and how, in years to come, I would use his example, when sticky situations would call for inspiration, to pull my courage through to the forefront.

I never remember seeing David again after that incident, though I never ever forgot him.

Tony and Jimmy had met twice before in combat, both occasions failing to reach a conclusion, both occasions left in 'mid-air' as it were. Due to these decisionless battles, a great hate for each other was still imminently alive and kicking. To put the hate to for good, they arranged a 'straightener'.

Tony 'the head' topped the scales at a robust twenty-one stone, with several hundred previous wins behind him. He had, though, in his time, been stabbed more times that a dressmaker's pin cushion and held many 'mars bars' to prove it, often displaying them for proof to disbelievers. One razor scar starts on the right side of his forehead, goes through his eyebrow, then starts again a millimetre below his eye and then runs two inches through his cheek where it meets with a multitude of other facial scars, each telling its own ugly story. Heavy, but solid and meticulously smart, inbred from years in the Royal Navy, he was rougher than sandpaper, but as handsome as a roving gypsy.

Jimmy was light at twelve stone, but punched harder than he should at this weight, knocking most of his opponents out. Funnily enough, though, Jimmy never usually fought with people unless they were members of the West Midlands Police Force. A peaked policeman's cap, to Jim, was a red rag to a bull. He hated 'the boys in blue' with a vengeance. Jimmy, with his brother Dave, were the kingpins in rough Holbrooks, where even the police went round in threes, (and that's in the station!).

Jimmy was, when he was sober, a lovely man: when he was drunk, he became a ribald fighting demon, who would capitulate to no man, very often fighting against whole gangs on his own, and still coming out on top. He was harder than a great big bag of hard things, making a scrapyard dog look like a poodle. Thin, wan face that held an unhealthy hue, capped by short, unkept hair, his hard eyes said, 'fuck off', no matter which way you looked at them (but only if he liked you). His brother Dave told me once that they played a Sunday afternoon game of rugger with all the other lads from the local, 'enter at you own risk', public house, where the ball, for seventy-five per cent of the game, lay forlorn and untouched in the middle of the field whilst the players had a free-for-all fight. Jimmy's team eventually won on account of the fact that their front runner was a brilliant burglar. They'd throw the ball to him and tell him it was a video, and you wouldn't see him for dust.

Jimmy's second for the fight was to be his brother, Dave (a very close friend of mine), a huge man at six foot five inches and sixteen stone, ten stone of which were in his 'shovel hands', whose unnatural strength was an absolute freak of nature. He once picked up a twenty stone man on the end of a builder's shovel.

Tony 'the head's' second was myself. Tony was working the door in 'Erections' nightclub, Jimmy worked the Pink Parrot, so they arranged to meet and fight on the forthcoming Saturday night, after working hours.

The grudge between the two had been burgeoning now for several years and started from an argument, which turned into a fight, between the two when Tony was working one of the City doors and was told to ask Jim to leave; Jim didn't want to leave. From there on in every time that they met they fought. This time, though, was to be the last, the decider.

Three a.m., Sunday Morning. The venue, Lady Herbert's Gardens. Then down into the Diplomat public house afterwards for a bevvie. Jimmy and Tony had both been fit men, pugilists of good standing, but with one thing and another, their fitness had dwindled and dissipated, eroded over the years, by far too good a living. Tony with his beer and curries, Jimmy with his beer and . . . his beer. They both had a week to find some sort of shape. In a week, all they would find is how bad their shape was, and how stiff those fucking exercises made you. Both shared restless nights and moody quarrels with their close ones, both couldn't wait to get it over and done with.

Tony's brow was etched with the memory of how powerful Jimmy's punches were from the last confrontation. Jimmy still had holes in his face from where Tony had bitten him. Both knew they were in for a hard time. Jimmy thought he'd take the title with his punching prowess and the fact that Tony was overweight. Tony thought he'd win on account of the fact that he was heavier than Jimmy, and Jimmy was undernourished and unfit. Both knew each other's strengths and weaknesses. Saturday night/Sunday morning would tell.

Lady Herbert's Gardens lay almost hidden down a quaint side street on the very edge of town called Chantry place, cornered in by Cook Street, almost on the back doorstep of the once popular Coventry Theatre, now a bingo hall. Once the podium of mega performers like Freddie Starr and Frankie Howerd, now holding stage to Fred Bloggs the bingo caller and a family of dancing balls. The gardens were surrounded in their entirety by a three foot high, grey stone wall, greening with age, occasionally splaying into the once splendoured gateways. Here, where the gentry of yesteryear strolled, was now the home to the city's offscourings in the shape of tramps and winos, Coventry's lost, nay forgotten, people. Inside was a well kept, half acre of resplendid gardens, long winding stone paths, cutting through it like veins through a leaf. Blossoms, cedars, oaks, rose bushes, families of daffs living together without prejudice, looking, in this concreteness, like a pearl in a bed of coal.

I was to be Tony's second, to hold his coat and jewellery and to watch his back should things get out of hand. Dave was to be Jimmy's second. It was one of the most awkward scenarios I have ever found myself in because I was good friends with both fighters, really I didn't want to be there.

Half a dozen of the 'Parrot' doormen came along to spectate, all uniform in bulk and occupation.

The moonlight shone down on the pair as they squared off, the dew, damp grass smelling sweet and fresh. The rest of us stood back by the miniature, red brick, summer house, now veiled in twentieth century graffiti, like a moustache on the Mona Lisa. Crawler branches clothed its exterior like the hugging arms of a protective mother draped around her over-protected child. At the back of Tony and Jimmy, a small feline blossom tree was guarded sentry-like by two huge cedars, an assortment of trees and bushes spectating with only the backdrop of the Swanswell Ringway, letting you know that this is Coventry city centre and not a picturesque country cottage in half an acre of sigh-inspiring nature. To their right, the roof of Lady Herbert's cottage rose above the century old stone wall that moats it like a protective cloak of armour and covered in green foliage. Rising high above that, some of the centre's high rise buildings overlooked regally by one the city's famous three spires. The Lady of the cottage would surely have turned in her grave if she knew her precious gardens had been turned into an outdoor arena for a blood and snot fight between two of Coventry's best.

The tension grew to grotesque proportions as the two circled each other, the beauty of the gardens lost to this barbarous spectacle. I felt a deep sadness inside me, watching my two friends prepare to batter the fuck out of each other, but it had to be done. The rivalry between the pair had been burgeoning now for three years, this they agreed would be the final encounter, at the end of which hands would be shaken.

Jimmy started the ball rolling by throwing a couple of jabs that fell short of the target. Jimmy's guard was high and tense, Tony's at half mast and relaxed. None of the spectators cheered or encouraged, all knew both parties and though they had greater loyalties to one side or another, all also had enough respect for both sides to keep schtum.

Jimmy threw a jab/cross, connecting sharply with the cross on Tony's right cheek bone. This was the opening Tony was waiting for. He rushed forward as Jimmy's right recoiled into grappling range, grabbing Jimmy hard and pushing him back several feet, slamming three solid head butts into Jimmy's face and then tucking his head away from the short punches Jimmy countered with.

Jimmy seemed unperturbed by the butts, but his face was gnarled with fear, anger and exhaustion. Tony was also sucking in air like there was a great shortage.

Twenty seconds into the fight and both men were exhausted. So far it was an unusually clean fight, no biting or eye gouging. Both fighters showing the other a lot of respect. Still locked in a grappler's embrace by the Lady's stone wall, Tony whispered something inaudible to our ears and they both parted, moved back to the centre of the green ring and again encircled each other. Jimmy shot out a stiff jab, then again a jab cross, connecting but not heavily. Again Tony, using his eight stone weight advantage, rushed forward, breaking down the distance and grabbing Jimmy, throwing him to the floor. Tony knew Jimmy was too good to box with, so opted every time for his strong point and Jimmy's weak point, grappling distance.

As they landed on the dew-sodden grass, the wind oofed out of Jimmy. Twenty stone is a lot of weight to have falling on top of you. Jimmy's fitness was bad, but his will was strong. He wouldn't give in, he let Tony know by sinking his teeth in his cheek. Tony just managed to pull his head away before Jimmy's jaws locked tight: 'Bang!' as he let him have another butt in the face. Another deadlock. Jimmy couldn't get Tony off, but Tony couldn't finish Jimmy off.

Again Tony whispered something to Jimmy and they stood up and squared off once more, both dying from exhaustion. Jimmy's face looked red and blotchy, Tony's the same, with his usually smart, side parted hair hanging lankly in his face. Jimmy now lacked the stamina to take advantage of this fact. Jimmy threw a half-hearted jab, but the lack of speed and fitness betrayed him and Tony, for the third time, sought the sanctuary of grappling range. They again fell heavily to the ground. After a few seconds of embraced inactivity, Tony whispered something to Jimmy, and for the last time, the two tired, bedraggled men rose to their feet, shook hands and embraced, both glad that it was over.

The feud was dead and a strong friendship and respect was born, as is often the case with such matters. Both seemed disappointed with their own performances, some who watched also seemed disappointed. Myself, I knew that when two 'class' fighters get together, they more often than not neutralise each other and the performance is often lacklustre.

What I really admired was the courage of both to do it the man's way.

8. Love On The Door

I had loved working B's and probably, at one time, I'd have worked there for nothing. It was great: the people, the atmosphere, the music, the scantily dressed, teasing beauties who made love to you with their eyes, the feeling of belonging, the camaraderie and K.T., especially K.T. She only frequented the establishment a couple of times a week, but that was enough to keep me going. She never had set nights, so every night I worked was exciting, just waiting and hoping for her to arrive. Pedantic Monday became exciting Saturday if she turned up, and time would go faster than a March hare on speed.

She was the most alluring, pretty creature, with a quite shy voice and unopposing nature. Gorgeously pretty face with deep, sparkling, sea-green eyes and shoulder length, corn light hair. An ever-so-slight lisp in her voice made her seem both vulnerable and sexy. Petite at five foot four inches with a firm, slight figure that was modestly veiled in a baggy, white blouse and geni slacks, that invitingly showed just the slightest hint of scanty pants underneath. Just looking was heaven, (I can't lie to you, I liked her). She always arrived in a group of four or five of her student nurse friends, she too was a student nurse at Walsgrave Hospital.

Nurses, nurses, nurses. Just the name conjures up vivid pictures of tight figure-hugging white uniforms and bed baths. I must admit, I've got a thing for nurses' uniforms, (but at thirteen stone, I doubt that I'd ever get one to fit me).

At first with K.T. it was just eye contact, then a casual 'hello', then, having broken the shell of her shyness, polite conversation. Quite often I'd offer to let her in the club free, mostly she declined. I liked her for that. The polite conversation grew to deep, long talks and confiding revelations. I was going through a bad patch in my marriage at the time and a confident was nice, not that I'm trying to justify what was happening, but sometimes you need a shoulder to cry on. Eventually I asked her, one night, for a slow dance at the end of the evening. She declined.

"You're married, it wouldn't be right," she said quietly.

"You've got a boyfriend as well, K.T., I only want to dance, not elope with you."

At this, some four months after our first meeting, we shared an embrace that was as close as two people can be and danced slowly, ever so slowly to, 'The Greatest Love of All', by Whitney Houston. Her firm, warm body moved ever closer in time with the music (K.T.'s not Whitney's). My body tingled at the feeling of her thighs, stomach and breasts as they contoured with my own body. I felt the hotness of her face as it touched mine. Our lips met, her mouth opened invitingly, and we slowly, erotically kissed for the duration of the record. Our eyes closed, shutting out the world. Closing our minds to the wrong we were doing, the sin we were committing, to the reality that would hit us so hard at the end of a record that was etching itself into our minds to stay there forever as a beautiful memory; a memory to be recalled and mentally recounted when life sucked and over-powering, unwanted spouses nagged us into oblivion, or when life's mundane groove bored us senseless; a video to be played over and over again when life becomes a stagnant pool of ordinariness. The record did end. Our eyes met on the crowded dance floor for a second that lasted forever, then she looked slowly and shyly to the floor, our embrace reluctantly broke and we parted.

"I think that was a beautiful dance," she said quietly. Then paused for a second, wanting and at the same time not wanting to tell me what she was thinking. Knowing if she did, that it could/would lead on to greater things.

A beautiful relationship with me, it would be, she knew, but it would be a delicate rose with the complication of many thorns. She dropped her eyes to the floor, hesitated;

"The rest of my thoughts are X-rated. I'd better go before I do something I regret," she said sadly.

She walked off the dance floor and re-joined the company of her friends. I let her go, though it was hard (it wasn't the only thing that was hard). The moment seemed too beautiful to spoil, and . . . I was frightened of those thorns too.

As she left, fifteen minutes later, I tried to stop her, to speak to her, though I didn't know what I wanted to say. She had tears in her eyes as she gently pulled away from me, so I didn't give chase, just stood amidst a swamp of confused thoughts and counter thoughts. One of her friends at the tail end of the leaving procession noticed my dismay, and stopped briefly to console me. She was a thin girl in her early twenties with dark hair and an attractive face, one side of which was paralysed due to an unfortunate car accident that left her speaking through the corner of her mouth, as though she was telling you a secret. The first time she ever spoke to me, I thought she was, until I noticed that she spoke to everyone the same way.

'Can't be much of a secret,' I thought. 'She's telling everyone about it'.

"Don't worry," said the secret teller. "She'll be alright." I feigned a smile.

"Do you think it's wrong, you know, me and K.T.?" I asked, knowing it was. She sighed and shrugged her shoulders.

"I don't know what's right or wrong any more."

At this she also left. I felt sad inside, yet happy and excited. The next few days found me in a world of my own, K.T. on my mind. 'The Greatest Love of All' seemed to be getting an awful lot of airplay on the radio. The thoughts of her stuck in my mind like glue. My wife knew something was wrong, because I wasn't arguing as good as I usually did. My workmates knew as well, because I was working hard for a change. I told them I was just on a bit of a downer.

Monday, Tuesday and Wednesday went slower than a flat-tyred milk float. No K.T. Everybody else in the world and his dog came into B's nightclub, but not her. I saw her friends and spoke to the 'secret teller', she just said K.T. was busy. (Fucking busy? What does that mean?) I gave her the extended version of Whitney Houston's 'The Greatest Love of All', and asked her to let K.T. have it. I hoped beyond hope that she would try to contact me. By Friday it all became too much for me, so I found out what number her room was at the hospital and visited her.

The nurses' home was newly built with the splendid Walsgrave Hospital that boasted swimming pool, squash courts and tennis courts as well as leisure rooms and even a public bar en-site for the staff, (it had a few old rooms for sick people too!), none of which compensated for the very poor pay the people of this profession received. 'Angels' is absolutely the right word for the nurses who are tireless and brilliant at a job that is thankless and financially rewardless.

The nurses' home was a three storeyed, L-shaped building that housed several hundred rooms for the nurses who came from far and wide. The building was modern with much glass. Glass double doors on entrance and huge glass reception windows. I opened the doors and made my way inside. It was four-thirty on the Friday afternoon. I finished work a little early so as to pay K.T. a visit. I didn't know what kind of reception she would give me, perhaps in the cold sober light of day she might tell me to 'fuck off', or perhaps, I hoped, she might fling her arms around me and welcome me gladly. Either way I wanted to see her. My mind wouldn't rest until I had.

I climbed the open plan staircase to the second floor with baited anticipation. The smell of polished floors hung in my nostrils. What should I say? Would I be able to control myself if she was in her nurse's uniform? I doubted it. I pushed the thoughts out of my head and made my way down the well lit corridor that had rooms to the left and right. 102. I stood outside. Damn it, even her room door looked sexy. I lifted my hand to knock, then paused and bit my lip. What should I say when she opens it? I lifted my hand again, opting to ad lib.

'Knock, knock'. I stood back ready.

No answer.

I knocked again, waited, still no answer. Just as I was about to knock for the third time, the door opened behind me. It was one of K.T.'s friends.

"Oh, hello," she said. I was embarrassed.

"Hello," I replied.

"She's gone to Southampton for the week, to see her parents." (Apparently they lived in Coventry, but looked better from Southampton.)

"Oh!", was all I could muster.

"Do you want a pen and paper to leave her a note?"

What a good idea.

"Yes please. If you wouldn't mind, that'd be great."

I can't remember what I wrote on the note exactly, but I do remember it was soppy and lovey-dovey. I didn't think I'd see her again anyway, so what the hell.

I slipped the note under her door, thanked her friend and hastily left.

Back at the nightclub, I still thought about her a lot, though not so much. I'd come to the conclusion that I wouldn't see her again and in a way I was glad, I was married to a nice person, though at that moment in time not happily, and it wouldn't have been right.

The queue to gain admittance to the club was as big as ever on this Wednesday night. I was searching people for weapons. Winston was to my left. I bent down to check the legs of the scruffy punk rocker in front of me for concealed weapons and the like. He was 'clean', though by the smell he was emitting, not in a personal hygiene sense.

As I rose, I caught a glimpse of her out of the corner of my eye, towards the back of the queue with a few of her friends. She smiled shyly, I ushered her forward, completely ignoring the unclean, 'clean' offscouring in front of me. She smiled and shook her head as she always did. I felt a great excitement inside me at seeing her. When she got to the front of the queue and inside the foyer, I took her by the hand and led her into the club, despite her quiet refusals. I could see she was flattered, her friends impressed. Her hand, warm and slightly shaky, made a feeble attempt to break free from mine. I gently squeezed it, holding it tight as I walked her to a corner so we could speak in private.

The club was dark and heaving with revellers. I found somewhere quiet so we could talk.

"Did you get my note?"

"Yes," she replied, shyly.

"I hope I never got you into trouble," I said, smiling.

"No, it's alright."

"I meant everything I said in it."

She feigned a smile and sighed a sad sigh.

"You're married, it's nor fair."

My eyes dropped. Quietly, I whispered,

"I know . . . I know."

"I won't be coming here again. I only came tonight because . . . well . . . because! This is my last time. It's wrong."

She held my hand tightly. My heart sank at her words, though deep down I knew she was right, and knew it was wrong. She pulled away and disappeared into the busy 'caved' nightclub. I mourned the rest of the night and gave her a wide berth, trying to make it easy for her, easier for me. At the very end of the evening, when everyone was leaving, K.T. lagged behind her friends a little as she walked passed me. I gently grabbed her arm; I knew she wanted me to stop her.

"K.T., can I have a word with you before you go?"

She gently pulled away from me.

"I've got to go, my friends are waiting."

I could tell she wanted to stop, to be with me, but knew that if she didn't go now and make a break from me, she may never be strong enough to do so again. I pulled her back to me again. She looked so beautiful, so inviting and yet so unattainable.

"K.T., K.T.," I said quietly and urgently, "please hear me out." She stopped trying to pull away.

"I know it's wrong, me and you. And I know I'm never going to see you again. I can live with that, but I have to tell you before you go that I love you."

She stared up at me fiercely as though offended, her beautiful green eyes began to smart with tears.

"That's stupid," she said. "How can you talk about love? How can you love me?" Her eyes began to stream, I held her two shoulders tightly and looked deeply into her eyes.

"I do love you, that's all I want you to know. I can live with never seeing you again, but not without telling you, K.T., that I love you."

I released my grip on her shoulders and she ran, crying, out of the club. I shook my head and my heart felt heavy. She was a beautiful girl.

That was the last time I saw her. Last I heard she was pregnant and about to get married to some lucky man. I hope that he appreciates her.

This episode happened during a particularly bad period before my divorce. I haven't included any details of the marriage because I know it would upset my ex-wife. I would also like to apologise to her for my side of the marriage failure and thank her for four beautiful children.

9. Instant Karma

The 'P' looked almost regal, though out of place sat on the edge of the dual carriageway'd Ansty Road, looking not unlike a small stately home. Three steps led up to a dual pillared porchway that had seen the ejection of many a disgruntled punter, usually bouncing off all three steps (if your aim was good) before coming to rest on the tarmac'd car park that was moated by a small nine inch perimeter wall. Opposite, front and side, were a few local shops and a petrol station.

The 'P', as the locals called the pub, was precariously set on the edge of the busy Ansty that cross roaded with the equally busy Sewell and Hipswell highways, regularly the scene of 'amber gambler' accidents, often these unfortunate incidents attracting not only a nosy crowd but also opportunist hot dog or quick food vans eager to make a fast buck.

At that particular time the 'P', according to reliable information from the managers, relief managers and bar cellar men, was a hot potato of a pub that few landlords were willing to take on. Its reputation was for uncontainable violence, frightening rather than attracting would-be tenants who gave it ever so wide a berth. The ones brave, or silly enough to climb aboard the 'P' virtually named their own price to a brewery who were only too glad to pay up. The pub did attract many scallywags, crooks, fighters and vagabonds, but in reality, it wasn't what I'd call a violent establishment. In fact, it was one of the nicest places I'd ever had the pleasure of working.

Due to its unpopularity with potential tenants and the aforementioned issue of acquiring suitable landlords, the brewery invariably placed relief managers in the pub almost by force. Nine times out of ten the reliefs were shitting themselves even before they set foot in the place. People of course, like dogs, sense fear and thus the neophyte manager attracts parasites and bullies like bees to a honey pot. The next thing you know the relief is no longer running the place: the punters are, pouring their own drinks, demanding protection money and eventually attracting more people of the same ilk, until the place is an absolute shit hole, and with each subsequent supplicating manager the reputation gets worse and worse.

The Potters Green Boys frequented the place with admirable regularity and, though lords of trouble, they rarely put fist to face in the 'P'. They respected, or were scared of, the doormen too much. There were around ten of them in all, aged between eighteen and twenty-two, and at their violent prime. Rarely did a night end without a fight, generally it was them who picked the said fight and even more generally with those they perceived to be weaker than themselves. Bullies is a good label for these people (though 'arseholes' would be more descriptive). They were mostly young boxers, so they had a certain amount of physical ability, but their main claim to fame was their involvement/ties with the infamous Bell Green Boys, who resided, as the crow flies, just a mile or so away from Potters Green in Bell Green. This association gave them, at least as they saw it, credence and their epistle to fame. In reality they were just young bullies whose purlieus took them no further than 'even number' fighting or simply, someone who would have a go back. ('Wankers' is, I believe, the correct term.) I, as one of the doorman at the 'P', neither liked nor disliked them. They were tolerated.

The leather interiored Granada Scorpio held Mr B's nine stone frame comfortably and easily. The 2.9 injection 'dream machine' was, in 1988, the status symbol of many a successful businessman. He smiled to himself as he cruised along the bottom of Hipswell Highway, Mozart dancing in his ears from his state of the art stereo system. He'd not had the car long, so the novelty hadn't yet worn off. As he neared the junction with the Ansty road the lights ahead changed to red and he began to slow, clipping his indicator onto 'right'. His intention was to head along the A4600 to the M69 and home, Earl Shilton, where his detached cottage in one acre of gardens held his heart, Helen. He'd not long rang her on the car phone to say that, at eight-thirty p.m., he was on his way home. Her soft, educated voice held tones of 'missing you' that pleased him. Fifteen to twenty minutes and he'd be home to her.

Some yards from the halting lights, he hardly noticed the six youths approaching the road from the right, preparing to cross. Mr B could not have known how violent the next few minutes were going to be, and how drastically they would change his life.

The Potters Green Boys had been on an 'all dayer'. Eight thirty-five p.m. and they were already smashed out of their skulls, and why not? They were celebrating. Johnny, with the shaved, 'look how hard I am' (and what a twat I look) hair cut, had just been released from 'the green' after serving six months for violence. As far as the 'Boys' were concerned Johnny was the man now. All day he'd regaled them with the hardships of rebarbative prison, and how stoically he'd handled it, and 'hey, it wasn't so bad, I'd do it all again'.

They actually envied him and dreamed of 'doing time' themselves. In reality, Johnny cried like a baby for the first three weeks, even cried silently for his mother and crept and licked arses so much for the 'six months' that the knees had worn out of his regulation prison trousers and his tongue was Khaki brown. At one point he'd even had to see the prison doctor for depression. The doctor took one look at his notes, ('wounding' on an elderly man), and told him, unsympathetically, to 'pull yourself together'. He swore to himself there and then that when he came out, he'd go straight. He couldn't bare to be locked up again.

The first day out he bumped into the lads, they treated him like a God, and after a couple of drinks in the Acorn pub, he started believing he was. Now, several hours and uncountable bottles of Pils later, he was trying, with his followers, to get across Hipswell highway to the 'P', if only this 'skinny cunt in the smart car would get out of his fucking way, who the fuck did he think he was anyway? I'll fucking show 'im'.

I was stood on the steps of the 'P' with Dave, a fellow doorman, watching the drunken yobs as they approached the road. I sensed something bad was going to happen. I nudged Dave who was busy day dreaming and pointed over at the youths.

"Hey, Dave, they're gonna kick off."

Dave followed my gaze, his hardy expression never changed. The esoteric 'mars bar' on the right side of his nose looked like a facial cleavage in the shadow of the early evening sun. He thought for a moment as though edging a bet.

"Yep, I'd say you're right, Geoff."

"Those fucking wankers kill me, look at them, they've been on it all day."

Dave turned to me with a look of concern. He was about forty, an old school doorman and had long since deadened the emotional nerve endings of apathy. He could see that mine were still sensitive.

"It's not your problem, Geoff, let them get on with it. No one will thank you for your trouble."

Johnny, with his very short, shaved blond hair, above a fat nose and narrow blue eyes, (the blue almost lost to the dilated pupils), began to swear and cuss at the car and its driver for no other reason than it was there and he didn't think it should be, and also he was trying to live up to the God image his mates had painted him with. Mr B inside looked visibly frightened. I left my podium on the pub steps and approached the perimeter wall, to get a better view, and assist if needs be.

Johnny was drunk and the cheering of his mates, as he kicked and punched the car, acted as a catalyst and sent him into a frenzy. As he got round the car to the driver's side, they realised he was getting out of hand and tried to stop him. He was almost foaming at the mouth, as he screamed in at the bewildered driver and punched his right fist clean through the driver's door window shattering the glass all over Mr B causing multiple cuts to his face, eyes and head. Somehow, even though he was being held back, he managed to drag the cowering Mr B, who was, he thought, surprisingly light, by his grey pinstripe jacket, from the car, hissing, spitting and cursing at the wan faced businessman who by now was scarlet with his own blood, and in a state of shock. From my vantage point he looked like a rag doll in the jaws of a Doberman.

Technically the situation was nothing to do with me and as I edged forward toward the affray Dave, my friend and fellow doorman, big built and slightly receding told me so and I hesitated. True, it wasn't actually happening on the grounds of the pub with whom I was employed, but on the other hand, an innocent man was being battered to a pulp, and for what? Driving a Granada (I could have understood it had it been a Yugo). Johnny was pulling and punching Mr B and Johnny's friends were pulling him, but to no avail. He had some how managed to drag his quarry some hundred feet, across the busy Ansty road and on to the grass central reservation. The battering was merciless, all the passing motorists seemed not to notice and carried on their merry way. All this had happened in seconds and I felt sick to the bone at the slaughter of this innocent man at the hands of this low life bastard with a fuck face and a dunce brain (I can't hide it, I didn't like him).

I could hear the ever so familiar, sickly smack of fist on face and the desperate grunts of the decimated Mr B. I could see saliva foaming around Johnny's grimacing face and smell the nauseating olfaction of fear as it wafted in to my nostrils. I had to do something, I couldn't stand it any more. I quickly ran across the road, careful to avoid the beeping cars. The anger was growing inside me like a tumour. Dave shook his head, he couldn't understand why I was getting involved, it was an unwritten rule in door work not to get involved in anything 'off the premises'. I couldn't help it though, I think I saw in that poor, innocent man myself as a school boy, unable to fight my own battles and, like him, at the mercy of those stronger.

As I reached the debacle the noise of violent cries, grunts and expletives rose high above the roar of the traffic. I managed to squeeze my hands through the mayhem of thrashing bodies and grab Johnny from the back, putting him into a rear choke hold and viciously ripping him off Mr B. As hard as could I squeezed my choke across his throat. I felt like I wanted to break the bastard's neck, my choke forcing a cackling noise from Johnny's throat as he gasped and snorted for air. His both hands, as is custom when you choke someone, leaving go their grip on the businessman and grabbing my arm in an attempt at assuaging the pain. I felt such a tremendous rage within me that I felt like killing him, destroying his being (thrashing him within an inch of his life as your dad might say); his friends still had a grip on him too.

Mr B slumped, semi-conscious, to the grass verge. He was in total shock.

Due to the fact that Johnny's mates were trying to get a grip of him at the same time as I was trying to strangle the life out of him, I was failing to get quite the grip that I was looking for.

"Fucking get your hands off him!" I bellowed at them. They all released their grip on Johnny as if he were on fire, then I released mine. Johnny turned to me half crouched holding his throat and gulping in air (you don't realise how nice it tastes until you haven't had any for a while). My fists bunched in anger as he stood straight and our eyes met. I challenged,

"Right, you fucking wanker, let's go. Me and you." He thought about it, he wasn't sure. I took advantage of his indecision and hammered home the nail or retribution.

"Fucking come on then, me and you. Go on, just give me one excuse and I'll fucking level ya."

I lined him up with my right hand, my adrenaline at fever pitch. He twitched as though forcing his redundant limbs to move. They refused, lack of moral fibre had placed them in the ranks of the unemployed. His mouth gaped open in shock, he looked at his mates, then back at me. His bottle was going at a rate of knots, I knew that I had him, but should I batter him anyway, even though he obviously didn't want to fight me? Should I smash him into unconsciousness? Give him some of the stuff that he had so mercilessly dished out on Mr B?

"You fucking wanker," I concluded. "Fuck off out of my face before I level you. Go on, fuck off." (I was in my 'F' word phase.) He scuttled off across the road, ashamed of his own cowardice. It was better really that I didn't hit him. If I did, he could have at least claimed to have 'had a go'. Better to send him away mentally defeated where excuses would hold no sanctuary for him. As Sun Tzu said in 'The Art of War',

'Hence to fight and conquer in all your battles is not supreme excellence; supreme excellence consists in breaking the enemy's resistance without fighting, then with his forces intact he will dispute the mastery of the empire, and thus, without losing a man, his triumph will be complete, this is the method of attacking by stratagem.'

His mates retreated to the pub and I helped a battered, bruised, bloody and bewildered Mr B back to his car. Diamonds of broken glass lay all around the road and the interior of his car. He was pale and debauched, he couldn't even speak. I don't think he even realised who I was and what I'd done. I felt a terrible apathy in my chest for this gentle distressed man, an apathy that Dave and others of his generation had learned to suppress due to familiarity. I made a mental note never to let my emotions become blunt to such dire situations.

A loud shattering smash, then another, shot my head around to find the bearer of the noise. Johnny 'Bottleless' was smashing in all the shop fronts across the road with bricks and fists. I watched as five young lads, (eighteen to twenty), tried to walk past him (how dare they?). He ran at them challenging and cussing, but they were just nice young lads, not out for trouble and they, understandably, ran away from him. Inside I smiled through my disgust. The act of smashing windows and challenging 'minnows' I knew would not heal the burning from his seared ego. He'd lost his bottle to me and nothing was going to assuage the pain from that. He felt like a wanker, and so he should, he was one.

By the time the ambulance and police car arrived, Johnny 'Bottleless' had disappeared. The ambulance took the much battered, much shocked, businessman to hospital, the police followed the trail of broken glass down Sewall Highway. Johnny had smashed several house windows en route, and with great struggle and even greater joy, they arrested him, sending him to jail. He got a measly nineteen months.

Mr B got much comfort from his wife Helen when he finally arrived home from hospital. He cried in her arms, she knew what a soft sensitive man he was and couldn't comprehend why anyone would want to hurt such a sweet, loving person. He took a month to physically recover enough to return to work, but to this day still hasn't completely recovered mentally, always conscious of the beating and the possibility of another.

He found a new route home, a little off the beaten track and a little longer, but it by-passed Coventry and that made it a little safer.

10. Retribution

I think it's fair and true to say that, 'what goes around, comes around'. Sometimes the gap for the said 'retribution' is short to immediate, others it is long to elongated. Rarely do 'Karma's' victims realise that the 'bad' they are receiving is directly or indirectly attributed to the 'bad' they have given, but in God's eyes it is and that's enough.

Peter was a B.A. degree student in Leamington's Mid-Warwickshire College. At twenty, he was in his second year and going strong. Thin and wiry with a keen sense of fun and a zest for life, he'd become very popular with the other students at the much populated college, and one of the four friends who like to frequent the night spots in Leamington, but only for fun, never trouble. He wasn't a fighter and hated violence.

The first I ever knew of this affable young man was when I saw a feature about him on Central News. He was no longer fun loving, no longer articulate. I felt extreme apathy as I watched my T.V. screen. His middle-aged mother and father, sad to tears, were helping him to walk through a Leamington park, his steps spasmodic, his mouth uncontrollably dribbling, his thin emaciated face the colour of ash, his eyes crossed and uncrossed uncontrollably. And then the screams . . . they cut through me like cheese wire.

The gut churning screams discharged from his moribund body with the simulacrum of lava exploding from an angry volcano. This once fun loving boy, the apple of his mother's eye, the jewel in his father's crown, the life and soul of the college parties, was . . . a cabbage. No more youthful badinage, he couldn't speak, he couldn't eat or drink on his own, nor hold his bowels, nor laugh, nor cry, only scream. That scream, as though his brain were reliving the terrifying night when his life, to all intents and purposes, ended with the swing of an unprovoked baseball bat outside a Leamington nightclub that he and his friend walked past on their way home. Ironically, they hadn't even been in the nightclub, they were just passing by.

As the story goes, the three doormen had gotten the worst of a situation within the club, and in an attempt to re-inflate their deflated egos, they armed themselves with bats and left the club to pursue their attackers, who had just left, and even the score. But it was too late, they were well gone.

Steve, the head doorman of the three, who was living in grey matter Siberia, wanted, no - needed, revenge. He had to hit someone, he knew he'd looked bad in the club and his ego was severely dented. As odd as it may seem this is a very common scenario, when people haven't got the courage to stand up to their peers they take it out on those below them. It may be their wives, children, or the first unfortunate person to pass by.

The three lads walking past the club this night were going 'to get some' for no other reason than 'they were there'.

Steve, grizzly faced and ugly with shoulders like Goliath moved towards the youths with malice in his eye. He needed an excuse, anything would do. One of them was laughing: 'what the fuck was he laughing at?' Steve's seething rotund face was angry red below his black hair, tied back in a pony tail. He spat the words out like sour milk,

"Oy, what's your fucking problem, what the fuck are you laughing at?"

The two other doormen, equal in size (XL) and stature followed behind. Steve swung the bat menacingly in front of him. Peter looked, not surprisingly, frightened, the fear locked him to the spot. He lifted his hands up in a capitulating manner,

"Look, we don't want any trouble, we're just walking past. Just leave us alone, why . . . ?"

'THUD!'

People in the busy nightclub heard the crack of the bat on the skull above the beat of the music, so loud was it. Outside, everybody felt rather than heard the hollow, sickly bludgeoning sound in their souls, and for years to come in their dreams as the bat cracked open Peter's skull and he fell into an unresponsive puddle of his own blood on the pavement. Everyone looked on in horror as an ever expanding pool of blood appeared around Peter's head.

For a long moment there was stark silence.

One of Peter's frightened friends quickly fell to his knees at his friend's side and frantically tried to revive him. Steve felt the overwhelming feeling of utter panic completely engross him, his partners in crime were dumbstruck.

"YOU'VE KILLED HIM, YOU'VE KILLED HIM, YOU'VE KILLED HIM."

Peter's friend shouted again and again. Steve and the other doormen ran back in the club hoping to find a little sanctuary; they were met by crowds of people leaving the club to find out what the horrific noise was.

The Ambulance men managed to save Peter's life, what was left of it.

Steve and his fellow 'armed' doormen, (I used the word doormen very loosely), were for their dirty deed imprisoned for three years.

Peter, he got life.

Three years in a cell of steel and stone.

Life in a cell of flesh and bone.

The Central News feature was highlighting the case and asking the dual questions,

'Why did it happen? And why were the sentences of the guilty three so lenient?' Three years in jail, out in twelve months with much crawling, arse licking and 'good behaviour', was hardly retribution.

The Pink Parrot nightclub in Coventry's city centre was probably the busiest and most popular of the several that the City housed. Certainly it was the newest, with dance floors that were spacious and crystal clean, bars and snack bars upstairs and down, the club holding, potentially, a couple of thousand people, with twelve doormen to control the whole issue. Twelve may not seem many, but each of the twelve were veteran, named doormen under the auspice's of Kev H., who was a gentleman, though very heavy in the city and further afield. A great leader of men, holding absolute respect from the doormen he captained, the management he worked for, and the 'punters' he controlled. A short stocky, handsome pitbull of a man.

The air in the club was alive with atmosphere, but as with all clubs stagnant with the odour of burning tobacco smoke. Passive smoking is a real pet hate of mine. In my car the sign on the passenger side dash reads, 'SMOK-ING KILLS!', so do I if you do it in my car'. The only time I don't mind passive smoking is if somebody's got a joint on, then I may get as close to them as lycra cycling shorts!

Steve and his two brain killing, brain dead mates, I was reliably informed, were in the club, strutting their wares. They'd only been out of prison a week, so were doing the rounds. There's something about a prison sentence that makes, or would seem to make, the ex-cons think they're hard. When they 'go down' many of them are whimpering cowards who can't fight sleep. When they're released, suddenly, miraculously they are fight-ers, tougher than a Soho scrubber and harder than sev-eral very hard things. Men to be respected, men to be feared, men to be looked up to.

'OH REALLY?' I don't think so. I think that they're the same people as they were when they went in except that now they've got a record, (and I don't mean 'Jail House Rock' by Elvis Presley) and a right forearm like Popeye (or a very close cell mate). Anyway, I never respected them, though I can't say I disliked them either, even though they were wankers and their deed against poor Peter a bad one. I felt no grudge, nor the need to equalise the situation by putting 'boots to bollocks'. I neither liked, nor disliked any of them. That is until they started acting up in the Pink Parrot nightclub.

We were alerted to the trouble by the sound of breaking glass, usually the first indication of trouble in a drinking establishment. We ran straight from reception into the busy club, filled to capacity with young, old, drunk, sober, thin, fat, smart, scruffy, pretty, handsome, ugly, smooching, dancing, drinking, joking people, all packed tightly into society's culture dish, the nightclub. Those who didn't move out of our way were, usually by accident, shoved out of our way as we raced to find the spanner in the works, the trouble.

On this occasion we didn't have to look far, it was happening just inside the club, by the downstairs dancefloor. The floor was round and sunken, surrounded by many soft, furnished chairs and tables. Everyone stopped and looked on in fascination as we went about our duties, separating thrashing bodies.

As I bent down to separate two violently embraced youths, (I hoped they weren't homosexual sado-masochistic lovers who were, by coincidence, doing their courting where the fight had started), I felt a sharp thud, then a deep tingling sensation to my right eye, where someone had punched me as I bent. I flipped and knocked him clean out with a punch that seemed to leave my body of its own volition, putting my attacker deep into sleepsville. He lay unconscious amidst two dozen trouncing feet on a beer sticky carpet that had seen more 'sleeping' bodies than a hospital ward. He was out of the game really before he was even in it.

Now I was incensed. My theory on separating fighting people is to do so with as little assault on them as is humanly possible. I wouldn't hit out or strike anyone unless the situation was beyond the purlieus of my restraining capabilities, or unless I got hit myself. I believe that if people are fighting in a club or pub, I as a doorman have no right to hit them for it, neither do I want to, only to eject them from the premises using a restraining hold with as little fuss as possible. Unless they hit me. My problem is that once I get hit, I lose it, and anything that moves after that is going to 'have some'. That may seem a little severe, it may seem like overkill, but it's not. It is merely a matter of survival: basically, the people you are dealing with, certainly as a doorman, make the rules, or dictate the pace. If they don't try to hit you, you don't try to hit them. However, if they do try to hit you, you have no choice (if you want to survive) but to hit them back. Once the first blow has been cast against yourself or a fellow doorman you forget all about restraints and hit anything that isn't wearing a dickie bow and moves. It's like a caged demon inside me, locked in with the key of justification, just sitting there waiting, I was hit, it was out. Running around like a Tasmanian devil. Someone came at me with fists flailing:

'BANG!' My right fist hammered into his advancing jaw and he was away.

Stewart, one of the other doormen, a huge man at seventeen stone, had lifted my first K.O. off the floor by putting his hands under his armpits, and was dragging him, like a sack of shit, out of the club.

"No, no, no!" Stewart shouted as I ran like a bull at the now regaining consciousness man, and head butted him back to sleep, and at the same time, knocking Stewart and the bloke he was carrying over and nearly knocking myself out. Instead of hitting his face with my head, I hit his head. I stood there for a few seconds and I saw stars floating around in front of me, and felt a numbing sensation in my head. I shook my head to clear it, dispersing the said stars, and looked around me.

There was one left, the other doormen had dragged the rest from the club and I was faced with the last of the bunch. It was Steve, the doorman who had 'batted' poor Peter. He was obviously nervous of me because I'd just K.O.'d his two underlings, one twice.

I approached him menacingly, oblivious to all the people around me. No noise, tunnel vision, just me and him. We stood face to face. I wanted to hit him straight away, give him no chances. He was bad and didn't deserve one. I felt as though I was out of myself, as though I was stood by the side of my own body looking on. Top athletes tell me that this out of body experience happens at the height of their career, where their bodies work themselves, finding the optimum movement for any given situation. It was a weird feeling of complete calmness as though I knew I was going to do the right thing. Buddhists call it the state of no mindness, 'into the soul, absolutely free from thoughts and emotion even the tiger finds no room to insert its fierce claws'.

Peter's mother wept as she sat in the solid tweed armchair and watched through the bay windows into the spacious back garden as her son, Peter, sat unresponding in his wheel chair, as his father threw him a tennis ball that landed on his lap and rolled back off. He, dad, picked it back up and tried again, unrelenting. All Peter's bodily functions had gone, 'irretrievably', the doctors had said. Surely nothing was irretrievable? Surely every avenue of recovery was worth searching? She couldn't give up on him. Could he hear when she spoke softly to him? See with his rolling, unfocussed eyes, his father trying desperately to gain a reaction from him? The constant incessant screams he emitted, were they of pain or were they an acknowledgement of his understanding that he knew they were trying and to please, hang on in there for him? Or was he as lifeless as his body dictated? Were they talking and throwing a ball to a lifeless body? Where was God now? How could the All Loving, All Forgiving let this happen? How could He let Peter, his mother and his father suffer so abominably, and the bastard who killed him (at least partially), escape with a year in prison, and then released? Where was his suffering? His punishment? Where was his retribution?

I didn't know it at the time and even now I'm not sure, but I think, believe his retribution was in my right fist as I bludgeoned him into the dark and lonely halls of unconsciousness. There he still lay as they carried him from the club, his face as colourless as chalk, and dumped him in the flower bed just outside, later to a hospital bed at Cov. and Warwick, where a fractured skull kept him for a week.

The Lord, if I may be so humble as to say, moves in mysterious ways.

11. Robbery At B's Nightclub

J was the cheekiest bastard on God's earth, but I can't lie to you, I liked him. He was a crook, fighter, thief and womaniser (those were just his good points), but he was very charismatic. My first meeting with the twenty-five year old was when he attempted a two a.m. robbery at B's nightclub. I happened to be working there at the time.

J was a tall lean fellow with a nose like ten boxers (it had felt more leather than a biker's arse), tidy mid-cut, mousy hair, and an affable gait that made a stranger feel like a friend and an old friend feel like a brother. He always had a beautiful girl on his arm and expensive clothes on his back, and he walked with a bounding confidence that told you 'he'd been there'.

Saturday night, one fifty-nine a.m., and this popular nightclub was buzzingly busy, lush with people, noise, smells and atmosphere. Walking from the reception area to the bar through so many bopping, silhouetted bodies could be a nightmare and if you were carrying a drink, forget it. B's was a wonderful nightclub moulded inside like a cave with a mini laser system that danced the revellers into a frenzy, a sunken dance floor that was never free from gyrating bodies and boys with 'desert disease' (wandering palms).

The tiny D.J. box was perched like an eagle's nest on the edge of the dance floor. This was usually manned by two D.J.'s, the Indian brothers Dan Singh and Wall Singh. Tonight, though, we were honoured by the presence of Richard Barnes playing to the tastes of the day and scanning the club for trouble or its potential. In the club the D.J. was the eyes and ears of the doorman: any problems, no matter how small, he would press the alarm.

On the evening in question, at two a.m., the night's takings were busily being counted by Dave, the handsome, smart, club manager, whose dark good looks attracted many admiring glances from the ladies and were met with polite, unreceptive nods.

Dave was a very charming and charismatic man, but his tastes leant slightly away from the women, if you see what I mean.

The small, cluttered manager's office was hooded in cigarette smoke. Dave, meticulously bandaged in grey suit, was counting the cash. Margaret, the lovely, bespectacled, pear shaped middle-aged receptionist was watching over him.

We, Colin 'no neck' Maynard, 'awesome' Anderson and Ricky 'jabber' James, stood behind the glass doors that separated the foyer from the club, getting ready for the five past two a.m. rush for the cloakroom, taxi and home. The night had been relatively quiet with only the one bit of domestic trouble between a fat girl and her thin boyfriend who were quarrelling over her 'supposed' romantic glances at another boy, which ended in her storming, nay waddling out of the club and him in hot pursuit.

John and I were, as usual, wrestling around the tiny cluttered cloakroom. I was the only one brave (stupid) enough to fight with him, underneath his rather deceiving apparel lay seventeen and a half inch biceps that had more crush than a boer constrictor and more venom than a viper. We had two cloakroom attendants ready to give out garments to the departing punters: one, a young Iranian student called 'Muhat Mucoat', and the other an elderly Scottish gentleman called 'Angus McOatup'.

The was a steady hum of mingling voices in the background. The D.J. had stopped playing the music at two a.m. on the dot: this was a very important thing for the D.J. because if he ran over, even by half a minute, he'd have the doormen on his back (judging from the love bites on the back of the neck of one of our D.J.'s I figure he may have enjoyed this), because when you've been working all night in a volatile environment, even a minute over is too long.

An hysterical scream from the office, just inside the partitioning glass doors of the club, stopped us at our play. It was Margaret, whose hips were as big as a pie shop (she had the kind of bottom that followed her like a wedding train). She screamed again and there was the sound of a commotion from the office.

Myself and the other doormen stormed through the glass doors and into the office to save her from whatever it was that was causing her to scream so loudly. The sight that met us was J with many, many bank notes sticking out of his bunched hands, and Margaret and Dave hanging from his frame like winter scarves in an Autumn gale. We were on him like a second skin, holding him tightly so that he couldn't escape.

"Alright lads, you've got me, it's a fair cop," he said. "Just give me a few digs and let me go."

All the doormen let go of him at once and looked at each other, (it seemed like a good deal to me).

"No," said Dave, indignantly, "I'm going to call the police. I want this reported."

We all shrugged our shoulders.

"Sorry mate," I offered, "he's the boss."

"Aw, come on lads, you know the crack, give us a few digs and let me go, you don't need to involve the law."

John gave him one of those looks that he's so fond of and grimaced his face (it scared me and I knew him). It was a hard look that said 'don't fuck', and very few did. I'm sure when he dies John will have inscribed on his grave stone, 'WHAT ARE YOU LOOKING AT?!'

"You 'eard what the man said, it's not our decision."

Ricky, black, six foot four, seventeen stone, shook his head and spoke in his high pitched voice, slightly slurring from hundreds of pro boxing bouts,

"Hey man, you done the crime, you do the time."

Ricky loved these one-liners. He was always telling disgruntled punters that he was going to "hit you so hard that you'll go back in time and when you wake up, man, your clothes will be out of fashion". The way Ricky hit them they'd be lucky to wake up at all.

Colin, who was wider than he was tall, shook his head in disgust. He had taken it all rather personally,

"I think we should give you a dig and call the police, this is B's, we've got a reputation to maintain." He poked J in the chest to underline his resolve. (Colin was like that.)

Margaret, visibly flushed, said something completely out of character, causing us all to turn and look at her:

"Bloody bastard!" This was the first time that she had ever openly come out on the doorman's side; she was forever scolding the lads for being 'too aggressive'. Her and Colin had an on going war of words, always culminating with Colin on the losing end of the verbal badinage and him telling her that he was going to 'batter your husband and son if they ever come down here'.

At this, and realising there was no other option, J tried to flee from the office by running straight through the doormen, more specifically through me.

'BANG!' He ran straight onto my right fist (it just happened to be there). I didn't plan to do it, nor did I want to do it, it just happened (honestly). I automatically followed up (as you do) with my right foot and kicked him right on the nose as he bent forward from the effect of the punch, busting it like a ripe tomato. (Now he had a nose like eleven boxers.)

Everybody 'oohed' in unison and sympathy as the blow landed, except J, who cupped his hands over the broken nose catching the blood as it issued from the wound. He stood up and looked straight at me, then winked (cheeky bastard).

"Nice one," he said. Then threw the cupped blood everywhere, over us, up the walls, on the desk, the chairs, and over Dave's lovely suit. Margaret screamed, Dave sat in his chair with that 'this really complicates matters' look on his face, and tried to wipe the blood off his clothes.

J then he cupped more and rubbed it over his face, ripped his own shirt wide open and ruffled up his hair. Ricky's mouth dropped agape. Colin's eyes nearly popped out of his head. I smiled (I admired his spontaneity). John drew heavily on his cigarette: this was his only reaction, his facial expressions rarely changed. I often wondered whether they were pencilled on.

In about thirty seconds, J, the affable opportunist thief, looked like he'd been machine gunned.

We all looked on in helpless dismay, as this clever, cheeky man threw himself into the corner of the room and shouted,

"Please, please, don't hit me no more, I've had enough."

Everyone else in the room looked on, helplessly dumb-founded. John and I walked out in disgust, while Colin grabbed J by the bloodied, ripped shirt and slung him into the leather seated chair and slapped his face to calm him down. J smiled at Colin, he knew that he'd got us.

The police were called.

In the half hour it took the police to arrive, J had banged his head and nose on the desk (oohhhh), and on the wall. He splattered more blood everywhere, (we all put on condoms in case the blood was contaminated), and generally beat himself up. Colin slapped his face once or twice but besides that we never laid another glove on him, all the damage was self-inflicted.

"What the fuck are we gonna do with this man, John? Why don't we just let him go, we don't need the police?" I asked.

"It's not up to us, Geoff. For me I'd give 'im a good dig and let him go. Dave wants the police involved. It's out of our hands."

"Do you think that the police will fall for his ploy?"

"They're stupid enough."

"What are we gonna tell them about 'ow he got the injuries?"

Rick and Colin walked through as I spoke.

"Tell them he done them himself. He did do most of them," Colin said.

"No man, they won't believe that," said Ricky.

"Just tell them the truth, he ran at me and I 'it 'im in self defence."

The lads all looked at me. Colin laughed.

"I don't think the law of self defence will stretch that far Geoff."

"Yea, but if we say 'e done the lot 'imself there's no way they're gonna believe us. I'll say I punched 'im and then 'e done the rest 'im self."

Finally we agreed. The fact that he was robbing the place and he did run at me should cover the fact that I hit him, or at least I thought so.

As the police turned the handle of the office door to enter, J sensing their arrival again threw himself onto the floor in the corner of the room, and again pleaded for mercy from a bewildered Colin who scratched his head in dismay.

The P.C. and W.P.C. tutted and shook their heads in disgust at the spectacle before them. They knew the crack, but J didn't care what they knew or how bad he looked because he knew that when the police statements were read out in court it would sound to a criminally uneducated jury like he'd been the victim of an unprovoked battering from four heavy set 'bouncers', bouncer being the operative word. The jury wouldn't see us as four young men with mothers and wives and children, with responsibilities and sensitivities, they wouldn't see our tears of dismay when our liberty is threatened, feel our fears of being maimed or killed 'on the door' by life's gratuitously Ramboesque minority, or hear our private sobs of despair as the penetrative lances of stress, fear, and aftermath pierce our very souls. All they would see is mindless thugs with an appetite for violence.

J was a very smart man. In his statement he told the police that he'd walked into the office by mistake, confusing it for the gents toilet which, coincidentally, lay directly opposite the office and that the doormen battered him for his mistake, making up the 'robbery' story to cover their (our) own backs. Of course the police didn't believe any of it but it wasn't for them to decide, it was for a jury in a court of law. The jury wouldn't be that stupid though . . . would they?

J was charged with attempted robbery, and six months later taken to Crown Court, where we, the doormen, were subpoenaed as witnesses. As I already said I'd originally agreed with the lads to admit hitting J in self-defence, because four rather sizeable doormen denying hitting J when he had obvious injuries wouldn't look too good in a court room. But, after reading Margaret's statement saying that none of the doormen hit J, I was forced to change my story and deny it also, or make her look like a liar.

The pine wooded court room hummed of polish and respectability. The twelve members of the jury, all uniform in their non descriptness, looked down into the court room with collective boredom.

J looked smart though still crooked in his 'court' suit. Some people have a wedding suit that they only wear for weddings, some people have funeral suits that they only wear for funerals, J had a court suit that he only wore for court cases. He'd walked these floors more times than the court cleaner, so many times in fact they were thinking of inviting him to the Christmas party.

The judge looked at us, the doormen, above his half-rimmed spectacles below the customary white wig. The defence and prosecution where oh so polite and oh so aloof. Prosecuting, defending and judging, within the realms of the law, and having no real knowledge of that which went on outside the purlieus of those four walls.

"I put it to you, Mr Thompson," drawled the skinny, lily-white, fragile defence lawyer, "that you struck my client hard in the face and knocked him to the ground, whereupon you struck him again several times with your fists."

"No," I said evenly, "all of his injuries were self-inflicted."

He tutted and shook his head, looked at the jury for effect and then back to me.

"And why, pray, would he want to do that?"

"Because he's a nutter," I replied honestly.

The jury burst out laughing, then stopped when the judge shot them a disapproving glance. This particular judge once sentenced a friend of mine to six months in prison for fighting.

"I could do six months standing on my head," said my cocky friend.

"Well, I'll add another three months on top, that'll give you time to get back on your feet again," replied the judge.

In theory, J's feet shouldn't have touched the ground, but his defence lawyer was good and then there was the M.D., giving evidence on his J's behalf, talking about how J's injuries were not conducive with being self inflicted.

The doctor was an elderly man, a police surgeon with more letters after his name than there were wrinkles on his neck, and the jury loved him. He was straight from the cast of a Hollywood court drama, educated, articulate, he must know what he's talking about.

Our story was basically factual. J attempted to steal money from the office and we caught him, the part about him pounding himself off the desk and walls was also the truth, it was only the one fraction about me hitting him that was erased from the storyline, for the reasons already mentioned.

As already stated J's story was right out of a comic book,

"Money? Never saw none your honour."

We said his broken nose was a result of him banging it off the desk.

J said we sat him in a chair and punched him.

The M.D. said,

"No! The cut on the nose is so shaped that it would have been impossible for the blow to have been delivered by forcing his own face in a downward motion onto the edge of the desk. More probably the blow came from above," he demonstrated with his hands as he spoke, "thus splitting his nose in the way it is."

He looked at the jury to add emphasis.

"This would indicate that the defendant was struck whilst in a sitting position by someone who, at the time of the blow, was standing up."

Sounds good, doesn't it, if I was in the jury, I would have gone for it too. There was only one problem: he was wrong.

The jury were baffled by this bullshit. They loved it. The M.D. obviously believed it too. But I knew it was wrong because I struck the blow (I was that soldier) and the said blow was upward and with a foot, not downward with a fist. He'd got it all wrong and didn't know, and I couldn't tell him. It made me wonder what the outcome would be if somebody's life depended on the forensics of this man? They wouldn't have a cat in hell's chance.

The M.D.'s theory on angular blows and their effect on the human anatomy (in this case the hooter) swung it for J and he got off with it, and fair play to him too. The jury thought they'd done a wonderful job until the judge read to them, as is customary after sentence, J's long, long list of previous convictions for robbery adding that he was due up in another court room in the same building that very day on another case of robbery.

They'd got it all wrong, they were as sick as pigs.

J looked as happy as a dog with two dicks. Myself and the other doormen were indifferent. We didn't want it to go to court in the first place. It just shows you, though, how the law works. Throughout the case it seemed more like we were on trial than J, still I guess that's our fault for being 'bouncers' and thugs. As doormen, that's the shade of light that you have to live under. Everyone loves you when there is trouble to sort, yet they hate you when there isn't. I read a nice ode once that was very apt;

'God and the old soldier all men adore in times of trouble but not before, when the enemy's gone and the wrong is righted God is forgotten and the old soldier slighted'.

12. Death On The Door

You push it to the back of your mind, try not to think about it. You avoid conversations on the matter, blank your ears when it's being talked about, close your eyes to the vignettes of death on T.V. and believe that it happens to others, but not to you. But, alas, in reality, the threat of dissolution (death) is a doorman's constant companion. It may only be on a subliminal level but it's there, it is his and his family's greatest worry, their greatest fear, death! The dark, macabre, oppressing state that eventually catches us all, some sooner, some later, but all are eventually enveloped by its dark mysterious cloak.

A doorman is a peacetime soldier, forever at death's mantle. Today he cuddles his children, tonight he grapples with fate, and you can't run from it, nor hide. Destiny and Karma, they are, when your time comes, your number's up, wherever you are.

A servant saw death in the crowd of a busy Bombay market place and he ran fearing for his life. He begged his master for money so that he may run away from 'death' to a place called Madras. His master reluctantly gave him the money and he departed. The master, obviously perturbed by his servant's dilemma, went to the Bombay market to seek out death.

"Why have you frightened my servant?" he asked death.

"Your servant should fear not," replied death, "for I have no business in Bombay, my business is tomorrow with a man in Madras!"

In the last five months in Coventry, eight people have been murdered (1992), several others have been maimed in shotgun, knife and other armed attacks, and the way things are looking, there are going to be more in the next few months, mainly in the guise of 'revenge attacks' on those formerly mentioned. I just hope that when the shit hits the fan, I'm not in the immediate vicinity.

In Coventry there are four main men, who have big and loyal followings. These four must, for obvious reasons, remain anonymous. All four of these men are good friends of mine, but, unfortunately, not good friends with each other. Over the last violent year in the city, all of these men, at one time or another, have fallen out with each other badly, causing mayhem and riots throughout the city, each coming back and counter coming back on each other in revenge attacks to prove a point, all fighting on the hill of power to become 'king' of the proverbial castle.

At the moment, the battle still ensues. When the bullets really start to fly, soon I think, there's a fair chance, because of the job I do and the friends I keep, that I'll be smack bang, right in the middle of it all, (ducking and diving 'Arry). But I can't and shan't complain. There is no sense in complaining. Life is a theatre of combat and the sooner people realise it, accept it and get on with it, the better. I will accept it, at least until fate deals me a better financial card and I can 'deal' out of the rat race and opt for a nice country cottage where I can live with my beautiful Sharon and write my books and plays and poems to my heart's content. I wait in hope.

Noel was nearly out of it too, so near that he could almost touch it, almost taste it. His life had been, in his twenty-three years, a hard one. Adopted as a half-cast child into a white family, growing up amidst much outside prejudice and confusion, never quite finding a friendly bed on which to lie. Adversity, though, had made him strong, tough and a fierce fighter. A tool he used readily to fight back hate and its ugly hand maiden, racism.

Though his gait was not that of a fighting man, his tall muscular frame, long curled Afro hair and handsome, almost pretty face put you more in mind of a male cat walk model than a pugilist. His fighting ability drew him to the door like a magnet, though like most doormen he realised it was a mug's game and wished he could do something else, with crime and violence burgeoning on undisciplined schools, a slack judicial system and terrible unemployment the job of 'bouncer' was the only thing blossoming in this otherwise barren, industryless garden we call Coventry.

Anyway, the women groupies that seemed to hang around most doormen made the job more than worthwhile, and then there was Gus and Tracey, his employers at the underground, student popular Dog and Trumpet. He'd have worked for them for nothing. They treated him like porcelain and gave him that sense of belonging that, up until now, had absolutely eluded him. He loved Gus and Tracey like he loved life. They filled a hollow in his heart that he thought would always lie gaping like an open wound. Gus and Tracey loved him back just as much, nothing was too much for Noel.

The previous New Year, Noel had turned up on their doorstep sad and dejected, almost in tears.

"I had nowhere else to go," he said, eyes smarting. They welcomed him regally, he became one of the family.

Gus often spent more quality time with Noel than he did with his petite, pretty wife Tracey. She often spent more quality time with Noel than she did with Gus. Camaraderie, love and a deep, friendship had grown between the three. Noel knew, as did Gus and Tracey, that he was no longer just an employee, he was family. His thanks for their kindness and affection came in the guise of guard dog loyalty and savage protectiveness towards the pair, never letting anyone talk down to Gus and absolutely pouncing on anyone who even so much as looked crossways at Tracey.

Then there was Roy, Noel's partner, and best friend, on the door who was handsome and rugged and a perfect partner in crime.

So much love, so many friends.

The one special girl in his life was Michelle. There were many female admirers in Noel's camp, but she was special. A pretty, white South African who was a student of performing arts. It was ironic really: Noel was black and Michelle's family were white South African, and yet they loved him, he got on with the whole family famously. But then that wasn't unusual, he seemed to hit if off with everyone, unless people crossed him. I watched him outside B's nightclub knock out two opponents in an instant when they started on him. His hands were fast.

The Dog and Trumpet was an underground warren type pub, in the middle of Coventry's city centre, which in the day seconded for a high quality eating place. The pool table was by the bar, and a cluttering of pinewood tables and chairs spread throughout the whole room which was spectatored by a railed balcony, just slightly higher than the rest of the room, that also held many tables and chairs.

Friday, 23rd April 1992. The pub was as busy as ever, mainly with students from the local Poly. They loved it here. They loved Noel and Roy too.

The Karaoke machine was playing as usual with many budding, would-be artists, (mostly piss artists), strutting their wares and singing their hearts out. Noel and Gus, much to everyone's delight, always finished the night singing duet to Noel's favourite song, 'Endless Love'. Noel sang the girl's part with a surprisingly good voice, Gus sang the man's part with an even more surprisingly good voice. It went down a bomb as it always did.

By the time all of the punters had left it was twelve-fifteen a.m., Saturday morning had just begun. Gus, Tracey, Roy and Noel sat around with many other staff for a quick drink and listened as Noel told them excitedly how his life was changing for the better. He'd just had a portfolio taken and had a great prospect of a modelling career ahead of him. Regular work with Gus and Tracey, good friends, a beautiful lady, life was sweet. They were all pleased for him, things were coming together and he never felt hollow any more. He was happy.

"See you round, fat man!" he shouted jovially at Gus as he left the pub with Roy.

"Not if I see you first, nigger!" Gus shouted back, laughing. They met up with Cam, Noel's close friend, who managed the Diplomat pub, and Marie, a friend of all three, and headed for the much popular Pink Parrot. After a short spell they decided to head for B's nightclub to finish off what had been a good night.

Around two a.m., Roy had had enough so decided to head for home. After a bit of play fighting at the door with Noel, Noel pushed Roy into the street and closed the door on him, laughing and joking that he was barred and couldn't come back in. Roy after much laughing at Noel's tomfoolery, wandered off to the taxi rank.

The street that held B's was starting to get busy. Many people were beginning to make their way out of the club to the taxi rank. Only a few yards out of the nightclub and to the left lay a take-away bar, a very popular late night chip shop. People milling backwards and forwards passed the rows of darkened, closed shops as though going on a midnight shopping spree. Cam, Noel's tall, smooth skinned, soft spoken Asian friend patted Noel on the back,

"I'm just going to run Marie and a couple of the others home. I'll be back in half an hour to pick you up," he told Noel.

"O.K., see you in a bit," Noel replied. At this, Cam left.

At around about the same time, Wayne, a local D.J., was just across the road from B's, and about to climb into a black cab with his lady. It had been a long night for him and he needed his bed. People didn't, he surmised, realise how stressful a D.J.'s job could be. Not only did you have to play, without a break, the music the punters wanted to hear, you also had to be the eyes and ears of the doormen, and also suffer the threats and indignations of the minority punter that he couldn't please with his record playing.

"Play, 'I Remember You, You Cunt', by Frank Sinatra and Sid Snot, or else . . ." Or,

"You haven't played the Nolans all night."

You can never please everyone.

'BANG!' An unsolicited dull thud that came from no-where (damn, I knew I should have played that Frank Sinatra and Sid Snot song), pummelled into the back of Wayne's head, sending a fuzzy feeling right through him. His girlfriend jumped back and screamed. Wayne was, admittedly, a D.J., but that didn't mean he couldn't look after himself. He turned, and though still semi-dazed, brutally showed his antagonist the pavement. The taxi, (nothing to do with me, guv), drove off so Wayne and his lady went back across the road to the club to try and find another, trying to work out why he had been attacked. Apparently there was no reason, he was just there. The taxi queue further up the road was far too long to wait in, and anyway, a few other lads were joining his attacker now, so he needed to get out of the way.

The scruffy, long haired youth dragged himself from the ground much to the amusement of his mates, who were mocking him on his defeat. By now there were a couple of hundred people around, most giggled or stared as they passed him. His pride was hurting like a hammered thumbnail so he ran across the road to the club to get Wayne. The doormen, in no uncertain terms, told him,

"To be on your way, good man."

"Fuck off you arseholes," came his reply, so they dragged him into the tight reception of B's and gave him a thraping, then threw him back out onto the street. His nondescript mates, collectively scruffy and arrogant, stopped laughing and started to goad and barrack the doormen. The doormen answered by closing the door on them. Completely by coincidence and on his own, Noel left the club to see if Cam had come back for him. He was still wearing his black and whites from his earlier stint at the Dog, and as far as the barracking lads across the road were concerned, he was a B's doorman. As one, they crossed over and stood around him. Noel was oblivious to what had gone on.

"You carrying, you got a knife?" The leader of the group asked.

"No," Noel replied, evenly. "I don't need one."

'THUD!'

Noel felt a dull thud, like a punch to his chest followed by a sharp penetrating pain. In an instant, they were upon him thrashing and kicking like a cheetah around a lame antelope.

Noel had been stabbed through the heart. Everything else was a dream, a myriad of thoughts and notions. His body plummeted to the floor only to be met by many frenzied, savage blows to his dying body, and kicks to his face. Everything was just a haze, there was a low buzzing that enveloped his whole being. He saw his friends in a dream-like frame, smiling before him: Gus, Tracey, Michelle, Cam, Roy, his mother, his family, all smiling, laughing, joking.

Then a bright light, then darkness, then again a bright light, and yet again darkness. Eerie, yet inviting voices, echoing voices shouting his name,

"NOEL, Noel, NOEL, Noel", loudly then softly, loudly then softly. Fear, sadness, grief, he felt none, only a haziness that was as pleasant as it was numbing. And again, that bright, bright light that seemed to beckon him on, pulling his spirit from his body, then, resistance, reluctance to let go, to let it free. More voices, more faces and love, an absolute and overwhelming feeling of love that erased his resistance, erased his reluctance and released his spirit from his body towards the light, the love.

This wasn't dying, it was living, real living.

Above his own body now, he understood, really understood. He saw the flashing ambulance by the side of the road. The ambulance men were by a body, was that his body? People by the dozen looking on, some crying, some quietly and urgently chattering, some dumbfounded, all shocked, and a cocktail of humming voices speaking as one,

'Is he alright?' Is he dead? Who is it? It's Noel. Oh no it's Noel.'

He felt free and blissful. As his body was being lifted onto a stretcher a zapping pull yanked his spirit back into his body, back to the haziness, back to the faces, voices, light, dark, light, dark, people were crying openly now, a misty cinema screen spread his life out before him showing the ups, the downs, the highs, the lows, then, more flashing lights, the sound of fast traffic, more voices, pitch black, sheet white, pitch black, sheet white, darkness.

Then, a soothing, inviting, disembodied voice, not male, not female, just a voice that again pulled him from his body, beckoning him,

"NOEL, Noel, NOEL, Noel," high and low, high and low.

Then again, that bright light and a stairwayed tunnel. Someone at the end of the tunnel calling him, smiling, beckoning with her hand,

"Come on Noel," releasing him from his body like a baby from the comfort of its womb.

Dying is being born, now he knew, now he understood, life was purgatory, death was heaven, and life.

"He's dead!"

Doctors and nurses crowded around the cadaver of twenty-three year old Noel Darcy. Died from a single stab wound to the heart. A blanket was pulled over the body of a handsome, young man who was in the wrong place at the wrong time. Or, from God's point of view, I humbly believe, in the right place at the right time.

I'd never seen a dead body before. I went to the chapel of rest to see my first, it was Noel's. A small reception room was packed with doormen, friends and family, most crying, some to distraction. A friend was gone, a son was gone, a good man was gone. I was with Steve Cater, one of Coventry's finest doormen. We'd both come to pay tribute. I walked in to the chapel of rest with some trepidation, not quite knowing what to expect.

Noel was laid out like a wax dummy. We looked into the coffin and neither of us knew what to say. I never knew Noel as well as some but felt an affinity with a man that had walked the same dangerous path as I and had paid the ultimate price. I touched his leg in a gesture of fondness, the coldness made me shudder and I had to go. I made my excuses and left, the feelings of doom stayed with me for a long time and I found it hard to believe that he was dead.

I looked at those I loved around me and at my life in general and realised how lucky I was and that life was not a rehearsal, we could all be dead tomorrow and should make the best of every day, treating each as though it were our last: it may well be. It made me realise that tomorrow is to late to say 'sorry' or 'I love you' or to 'live life', to have the child you always wanted to have, change the job you hate so much, take the holiday that you've been meaning to take but have been 'too busy', too late to 'make amends', 'change', 'diet', 'train', 'have fun', whatever it is that you want to do, tomorrow may be too late. If there was one thing that I learned from Noel's death it was that life is precious, not even one single second should be wasted on futility. Life is an opportunity, an opportunity to achieve, to make friends, to live, and yet so many people settle for so little because they won't get off their arses. They are too lazy, or too frightened or too ignorant. Life is a beautiful car, a tank full of petrol and a journey. If you haven't got the 'balls' to use a little of the petrol and pull out in to the traffic you won't get to experience the journey. Too many people sit in the driveway of life with the engine off, dithering about whether to go this way or that. In the end they take the 'safe bet' and stay where they are, and live the rest of their lives 'in the driveway of life'. It's true that most people go to their graves with their best songs still in them.

Our Lady of Assumption church, Tile hill, Coventry.

The funeral of Noel Darcy was attended by hundreds of doormen, all dressed in the black and whites of the trade. Also hundreds of mourning friends arrived from all over to pay tribute to this very personable man. Noel's closest friends acted as pall bearers and carried the coffin. The vicar said that he had never known such a well attended funeral. It was absolute credit to Noel that so many people turned up to pay their last respects to a charismatic man who will be sadly missed by many.

13. Part Time Soldier,
and other humorous encounters

In a sea of violence it is often the humorous moments that act as your metaphoric life jacket and keep you afloat when all around are throwing in their hands and sinking.

G, six foot three, sixteen stones of sinewy muscle and a cauliflower face, was everything that you might expect a doorman to be: gum chewing, swaggering walk and a protruding chest. He was everything that I tried not to be; he was on the wrong side of confident, over confident, the by-product of this being arrogance. The T.A. to G and to many other 'part-timers' was just an ego extension. It amazed me that during the Middle East conflict many of the T.A. members (certainly the ones that I knew) were dropping out of the T.A. at a rate of knots with the 'bullet in the foot syndrome'. As soon as it became 'real' they were dropping like newspapered blue bottles, dreading the post every day in case they were 'called up', and the harsh reality of someone saying,

"O.K., we've done the theory bit, you've taken the pay and the trips abroad, now let's try it for real . . . What do you mean you don't want to play any more?"

Actually, G was quite handy, though with too much 'front' (more than Woolworths) and too little bottle (less than a redundant milkman). In a nutshell he was a fresh-man who thought he was a veteran. However, G was proud of being a 'weekend' (I thought that was what you got after five days of shagging) soldier and took every opportunity of tearing the arse out of it.

He came into B's one night with a couple of impres-sionable mates (also in the T.A. until the Middle East con-flict - 'got a bullet in me foot, Doctor'). He was showing

them around the town trying to impress them with what
and who he knew, (as you do). They were suitably impressed, that is until he pushed his luck a little too far.

A young lad and his equally juvenile lady were having a lovers' tiff (actually she was battering him) by the
crowded bar at the bottom end of this small but popular
night spot. The argument was getting a little out of hand,
so we, the doormen, intervened.

Try as we might we couldn't stop the young, aggressive female from shouting and threatening. Her coy boy
friend wasn't saying much in retaliation, he looked frightened and we surmised that she must have 'given him
some' before.

G had been watching from the bar only feet away, and
in his wisdom, decided that the doormen were handling
the situation wrong, all wrong. So, in an attempt at im-
pressing us and his T.A. mates, he decided to demon-
strate 'how it was done'.

Chest out, chewing gum to the beat of the music, he
swaggered across, through the crowds of onlookers, to
the altercation. He walked like John Wayne in 'True Grit'.

Pushing his way through he placed himself right in
front of the garrulous woman. She was a small girl at five
foot with a six foot three attitude and a seven foot mouth.
She wasn't pretty and I rather unkindly wondered if she'd
'uglied' for England? Her face looked like a knotted log.

G faced her and without provocation, without gesture,
handshake, nod, wink, no please, nor thank you, no kiss
my arse, nothing,

'SLAP!'

He just whacked her straight across the mouth with
the flat of his hand, leaving a glowing red hand print on
the side of her face. As his eyes turned to catch the acknowledgement and adoration of his T.A. mates, the toe
of her high heel black patent right shoe sent his testicles,
faster than a Porsche, into his stomach, and his heart,
equally as fast, into his mouth. For a second the only

things that moved were his eyeballs: they crossed inwards, followed by his mouth which dropped agape. Then as the pain of 'crushed nuts' (sounds like something you put on top of an ice cream) spread through his stomach he showed what he was made of by collapsing to the floor like a paper house in a rain storm. Everyone, with the exception of the young lady who was still trying to kick holes in him, fell about laughing.

When G finally found his shaky feet he walked, with a distinct crouch, back over to his mates who were having a hard time suppressing their laughter.

G's swagger had disappeared with his swallowed chewing gum and his chest had lost considerable inflation. Somehow he didn't look so big any more. Needless to say, for that night leastways, G remained humbly quiet. John 'Awesome' Anderson was looking on,

"Know what 'T.A.' stands for, Geoff?"

I didn't answer.

"Total Arsehole," he said, as he turned and walked away from the debacle.

I laughed until my stomach hurt the night that Barny and I ejected a 'woman possessed' from the same nightclub for fighting and being ugly (we could live with the former but the latter was intolerable).

Barny, so named because he was a facsimile of the Barny Rubble character in the 'Flintstones' cartoon, was a bodybuilder friend of mine who was short with a heavy and powerful physique and an equally rugged face. He was the strong man on the B's door (I was the nutcase).

The girl in question (I use the word 'girl' very loosely, 'Radio Rental' Rob nicknamed her 'bag of sick', though I don't know if she was 'brought up' in Coventry), had just given some lad in the club a thorough beating so we'd asked her kindly to vacate the premises. Her unsolicited 'FUCK OFF' (nice girl) meant that we had to remove her forcefully, much to her dislike, and my goodness she was a handful. She kicked, punched, scratched and bit, she was like a rabid dog (no disrespect intended to rabid dogs).

The whole screen was filled with knickers and torn tights, it was so undignified. Eventually we managed to throw her out. Now I know that to the reader this is all sounding a little Over The Top, because you tend to envisage a dainty little thing being man handled by 'bouncers'. If she were dainty you would have a valid point, but she wasn't. I wouldn't even describe her as a woman, she was a completely different species not commonly known to mankind and only found in the deepest, darkest recesses of the nightclub. Why, I often ask myself, are so many people wasting their time stalking the Yeti in Tibet and the Loch Ness Monster in Scotland? Come to B's, it's full of them.

Anyway, once the dirty deed was done we shut the red, steel-reinforced door and locked her out (or ourselves in, depending up on how you look at it). As soon as we had closed the door she started kicking and punching it and shouting unrepeatable profanities at us.

I watched her carefully through the spy hole in the door. She was a frightening sight. As soon as the abuse stopped and she moved away from the entrance I bravely swung it open, waggled my hips sexily and shouted,

"Hey, beautiful, I suppose a 'ride' is out of the question?"

Her face contorted into a domino of hate, making her previous ugliness look pretty by comparison. Barny thought that she might have been wearing a Halloween mask. I said that 'they didn't make them that good'.

Like a bullet from a gun she shot at me, legs and arms violently flailing like an exploding Catherine wheel. I just managed to get myself inside and the door shut before she reached and devoured me, the reinforced door taking the brunt of her onslaught.

By this stage Barny and I couldn't speak for laughing. The more she attacked the door the more we laughed, tears ran down my face in rivers and my stomach cramped. When I, we, finally calmed down and the attack up on the door had ceased I looked again through the spy hole in the door to see if the coast was clear. It was, or at least it seemed to be. We creaked open the door, me at the front and Barny close behind and peeped our heads carefully out.

She was nowhere to be seen, so we slowly crept out like two night burglars, looking this way and that for the demonic damsel. Still no sign. I walked right out the door with Barney sticking to me like a greased vest (I know that I was taking my life in my hands but that's the kind of guy that I am).

"Where is she?" I asked Barny, who shrugged his huge shoulders.

"I don't know, I can't see her."

"Ha, we've obviously scared her of."

"Are you sure?"

All the time that we spoke and scanned I could feel the uncontrollable urge to giggle rising in my stomach like a bad curry. There was no one in sight, only two lads about fifteen yards away to our right by the concrete staircase that led on to the roof-top car park above.

"YAAAAAAAA!"

The glass breaking battle-cry deafened us. We were temporarily rooted by fear to the very spot on which we stood. From her hiding place, crouched behind the two lads, she ran at us, like a Viking, stiletto in hand. Eyes wide in disbelief and mouths ajar with shock we, in our haste and laughing hysterically, turned, ran and tried to get back into the club, away from the storm that ensued.

The laws of expansion, not to be defied, said 'fuck off' and wouldn't let both Barny and I through the door at the same time, no matter what the danger. All the time that we struggled to get in the door she was getting closer. I could almost feel (taste) her breath on the back of my neck, the hairs stood on end, a cold shiver ran down my spine. Eventually, after what seemed like a lifetime, we managed to squeeze through, falling onto the floor with Barny falling straight on top of me, both crying with laughter as the door took a third pasting.

She did eventually 'go away' when Colin 'no neck Maynard' cooled her down with the fire extinguisher (I half expected her to melt in the trend of the 'wicked witch of the east' from 'The Wizard of Oz'). I was only glad that we didn't have to fight her. I'm sure we would have lost.

A lot of people like to take cheap shots and throw verbal gauntlets, when you're a soft spoken, mild mannered (damn good looking) fellow with an ever-so-slightly receding hair line (so slight that you may not even notice). You sort of set yourself up for it. Few of these antagonists see the funny side, though, when you retaliate. The two disillusioned lads from neighbouring Rugby proved to be no exception.

Both were tall and thin, one had a skinny, gaunt face and 'hand me down' apparel, the other a frowning, aggressive face and staring eyes. He seemed to be competing with his mate in the 'who can dress the scruffiest' stakes with an old grey jumper, and grey flannel slacks. Both looked in dire need of a fashion transplant, though twenty years ago they were probably trend setters.

The two left B's well before the end of the evening. Colin 'no neck' and I were stood, minding our own business, by the exit door as they passed on their way out. Neither looked very happy and thought they'd tell us why. We weren't really interested, but, they told us any way.

"We're from Rugby," (ah, that explains the clothes) said the gaunt one. "We came to B's tonight to have a good time, but we've had a crap night and it's all because this is a shit nightclub, in a shit city. We won't be back again!"

He poked aggressively at my chest to add emphasis, and spoke out of the corner of his mouth as though he was chewing straw. I was, to say the least, annoyed at his disrespectful, insulting manner.

"Why don't you fuck off back to Rugby then?" I like to try the polite approach first. "It's only a one horse town, and hey, you'd better hurry, they shut the gates and turn the lights off at twelve o' clock."

Colin laughed, the country yokels were not so amused. The gaunt one replied bitterly,

"It's a lot better than this shit hole."

I could tell that he was beginning to bite so, sure that I was on a home run, I struck again,

"Listen mate, there are only two things that ever come out of Rugby, steers and queers. I don't see any horns on you."

He thought for a moment about the implication, then when the penny dropped he started swearing and cursing at me. I just laughed. After a few seconds and feeling vindicated he and his 'jumble sale' friend turned and began walking away.

"I'll be back for you, you wanker!" he concluded.

I should have just let them go, really, but I couldn't, especially with Colin spurring me on.

"Hey mate!" As I shouted they both turned around. "Isn't your mother the local prostitute in Rugby?"

A cheap shot, I know, but I couldn't resist. He turned red and then green. He got so angry that he was struggling to get his words out. Frustrated at his verbal incompetence he resorted to the obvious 'physical' and ran at me only to be stopped by his mate who dived on top of him and forcefully held him back (gosh, wasn't I lucky?).

Colin and I burst out laughing, which just made him worse. He was almost foaming at the mouth and his eyes popped out of their sockets. His companion wrapped himself, like a blanket, around him until, finally, he calmed down. When he did and his mate persuaded him to 'leave it' they turned and began to walk away.

"I'll be back, you bastard! I'll have my day with you. You'll regret ever crossing me."

His attack was at me, I saw no point in trying to keep on his good side if he was going to be like that about it (mardy), so I went in for the kill. I placed my thumb and forefinger to my mouth, mocking deep thought, and said,

"Hey, it's your dad that's the pimp, isn't it?"

Oh my goodness, what had I done ? This really upset him. He turned all the colours of the rainbow and ran at me again like a man possessed, this time his friend had to practically fight with him to stop his one man crusade. My belly ached from laughing at the spectacle before me.

"YOU BASTARD, I'VE LOST BOTH MY PARENTS!"

Colin looked at me and then at the man from Rugby.

"Well! Losing one is bad enough," said Colin, "losing two is just downright careless."

"Don't worry, you're bound to find them when your cleaning up, they're probably down the back of the settee," I added.

"AAAARRRRRRRGGHHHH! YOU BASTARDS!"

He was angry, I could tell. He got so mad now that he was starting to foam at the mouth. He tried to wrestle free from his mate to get at us, his mate was getting a little fed up with trying to hold him back.

"FUCK IT!" he shouted, letting the brothel keeper's son go. "If you want to fight with him, do it, I'm sick of trying to hold you back."

At this he tried to rush forward at me to no avail. Lack of moral fibre had glued his feet to the ground, his bottle left him via the back entrance, he had just discovered that adrenaline was brown.

"Come on then, what's the matter with you? Your mate's not holding you back any more." I knew he wouldn't fight.

"I'll come back another time, I won't forget this."

"Yea, sure, I'll be waiting, ask for me by name, it's Geoff Thompson."

He nodded his head, as these people do, and disappeared up his own arsehole.

My hair, or lack thereof, has always been a source of mock and ridicule for potential antagonists, something that I've had to learn to live with (or in fact without). I'm not sure whether the people that feel they have to mention it really mean it as a direct insult or not, though when someone calls you a 'baldy bastard' it's not easy to take it any other way.

I have learnt over the years to weather these insults and also expertly to counter them when the opportunity presents itself. It annoys me terribly, though, when the gauntlet throwers respond so negatively to the said 'counters', usually in reference to their 'warts' or fat hips. After all, it was them that started it. People love to be smart and give it out but none seem keen to 'take it'. Some, though, are a little too quick for me to get back.

One night I'd thrown a lad out of the nightclub for being ugly and scaring the women (only joking, he was stealing hand bags). He walked a safe distance from the door and in front of a large appreciative crowd shouted,

"OY! BALDY! DIDN'T ANYONE TELL YOU THAT RECEDING HAIRLINES ARE OUT?"

Even I had to laugh at his cheek.

A particular stout man who was bigger than a pie shop passed me on his exit from the nightclub, trailing two stone of buttocks. He had two pretty ladies on his arm who he thought he might impress at my expense.

"Hey chap," he quipped, pointing at my depleting hairline, "you want to have a word with your hairdresser."

"And you want to have a word with your dietitian, you fat bastard," I said quickly.

He coloured up and his two lady friends went into fits of laughter.

"What a blow out!" one of them said, through gulps of laughter as the fat man beat a hasty exit.

I can also clearly remember, as though it were yesterday, (oh yea, it was yesterday) the smarmy woman (she was one of many) who tried a similar dirty trick in a bid to gain a cheap laugh with her friends, again at my expense. Now I don't mind people having a laugh at my expense if it stays within the realms of good taste or, alternatively, if I know them, but when complete strangers feel compelled to tell me that I'm baldy I find it disrespectful and do take offence. To be honest it's very hurtful.

On this particular occasion I was working at the Diplomat pub in Coventry city centre. It was near the end of the evening and I was asking people, ever so politely, to see their drinks off. I approached a group of about half dozen lads and ladies, and in a voice that would have made Gandhi sound aggressive I asked them would they mind drinking up their drinks as it was time for us to close. Myself and my request were blanked completely. The aforementioned 'ugly bitch', who was a member of the group, not happy enough with the fact that I had been totally ignored, thought she'd add her 'two penneth'. She looked me up and down belittlingly, then looked at my head and lack of hair, pondered for a second, then announced to me and the people who were in hearing range of her fog horn voice (about two square miles),

"You're losing your hair!"

(Ahh. So that's what that bald patch is on my head). I felt embarrassed and humiliated, though I didn't let her see. All the same my honour needed defending so I 'defended' in the only way I knew how.

"It could be worse," I replied, looking her up and down like a smelly subservient (no disrespect meant to smelly subservients), "I could be a right fat bitch!"

The whole group went deathly silent.

"And if you're so concerned about my lack of hair how about donating a bit off the top of your lip?"

She went very quiet (I preferred her that way) and I walked away before she could think of an even smarter reply. Of course I know that sounds a little impolite but people in glass houses shouldn't throw stones.

Drunken women, I mean no offence when I say this, are the very worst when it comes to taking cheap shots, telling you unreservedly and matter of factly what they think of you or parts of your anatomy, in my case the dreaded 'receding hair line'. I always, always have the last laugh on these disrespectful people with my uncanny knack for observing faults in people and hitting nerves with sharp, wicked replies to unsolicited verbal attacks upon my person, that cut to the bone,

"Goodnight, fat arse!" being a particular favourite as they leave the pub at the end of the evening, or,

"There's no need to take it out on me just because you're flat chested!"

Or even,

"You smell nice. Have you been sick?"

I'm not a naturally vindictive person (I've had to practice very hard to get this good), but when people verbally attack me for no reason and with the sole intention of embarrassing me, then I will let go, verbally, with no holds barred. Believe me, it hurts them a lot more than it does me. Women, especially, hate being reminded of cellulite, flat chests, big noses, moustaches etc. But, if they insist on reminding me of lack of hair, then I feel obliged to discard a few home truths in retaliation (it's only fair).

I've always admired wit and certainly it does seem to be a by product of working in the 'people business', though the humour is often very black (isn't all the best humour?). One doorman that I knew even carried his wit into the county court with him. He'd just been sentenced to six months in prison for a fighting offence.

"Have you anything to say?" asked the sour mouthed Judge.

Cool as you like, Mr Wit reached into his inside jacket pocket and casually removed a silver cigarette case, flicked it open, raised it to his mouth and spoke into it in an exaggerated American voice,

"Beam me up Scotty!"

The whole court room, barring of course the Judge who remained stony faced, flared into a crescendo of laughter. For his insubordinance the Judge added a further eight weeks onto the end of Mr Wits sentence. A small price to pay, I think, for such a classic show of brave wit.

Epilogue

Today, 15th June 1992, as coincidence would have it, 'Watch My Back - A Bouncer's Story', goes to print, and today I finished the last chapter of the sequel, 'Bouncer'. If people are kind, interested or curious enough to buy 'Watch My Back' and it's a commercial success, then this book should hopefully follow in its footsteps to the publishers, printers and bookshops. If 'Watch My Back' does not succeed, then this will probably by-pass all three on its way to my bedroom shelf, where I'll, no doubt, give it an annual dusting down and talk about the time that I nearly became a writer. I pray that it's the former rather than the latter.

At the time of writing this book I am still working on the Devon door under the auspices of the charismatic Seymore, a gentleman/fighter of great standing. In the day I am conscientiously trying to earn my living as a writer. Still in my beautiful little house, with my beautiful Sharon, who is behind me one hundred per cent. I've said it for the last six months and I'll say it again now. 1992 is my year, I believe this year will bring me success in some shape or form. Happiness I do not seek, because I have it by the barrow load and I thank God for it. I love God. He has given me Sharon and my four beautiful children, Kerry (fourteen), Lisa (twelve), Jennie (nine) and beautiful Louis (three), (named after Joe Louis the boxer), and more chances than I deserve. Credit where it's due, thank you God.

Violence is burgeoning in society, though in my own life it is becoming a much smaller part. For the former I am sad, the latter, I am extremely grateful. Ultimately Karate teaches its practitioners to transcend violence, suppress the ego and checkmate pride (I am now able to let people call me 'baldy' twice before I hit them). I'm maturing as a Karateka and as a person, because all three are on my curriculum and I intend, eventually, to lose them from my life. Like most people I still feel the pain of life and my own weaknesses, though Karate has taught me to handle it more stoically.

As a doorman I have learned how to administer violence as brutally as is deemed appropriate. I have also learned to replace it with guile when and wherever possible.

I smile when I watch the romanticised, celluloid vignettes of fighting and violence because they make it look easy when really it is extremely hard. They make it look fun when really it is frightening. They make it seem 'good' when really it is evil, they make you want to be there when in reality, if it happens to you, it is the very last place on earth that you want to be. If you are ever in front of a violent situation that is about to erupt believe me when I tell you that you'll feel like 'shitting' yourself, anyone that tells you any different is a liar. It's an awful billet to find yourself in, over-exposure also has a lasting negative effect on the human mind, involvement in extreme violence has, at times, made me feel slightly mentally unstable: sleeping, eating and drinking violence, lining up everyone and anyone as a matter of course and thinking the kind of barbaric thoughts that should enter no human being's head. Often I wondered if I would ever be able to pull myself from its evil grip? I have, but it's been a bastard.

When exerting your brain to reach higher planes of understanding and control, it is very easy for exertion to become over-exertion and stability to slip into instability, for, to reach these higher planes you have, ultimately, to push yourself through such excruciating pain and endurance that the very 'mind' you are striving to gain complete control over, 'aborts' and you lose complete control, so beware.

The law of Karma, 'A good for a good, a bad for a bad', is not a rule to play around with. Be assured that every unjustifiable 'bad' you do will be repaid, as will every 'good'. So, unless justification is your ally don't do it, and Karma will have no quarrel with you. If there is one thing that Karate and the 'door' has taught, it is that life should be about making friends and not enemies, about lightening your Karmanic bag with good deeds rather than weighing it down with dirty deeds.

Enlightenment, as developed by facing extreme adversity, has enabled me to attain a YIN/YANG (hard/soft-dark/light) personality that will only employ violence as a last resort, storing the venom inside like a Camel might store food in its hump to regurgitate when and if the need arises. I am, then, ninety-nine per cent gentleman, one per cent animal. If a man knocks on my door for a helping hand with a broken down car I will think nothing of helping him out, however, if a man knocks on my door for trouble and Karma is with me, I will think nothing of biting off his nose and spitting it down his fucking throat.

To all of you out there kind enough to read my ramblings I thank you very much and wish you well, to all those out there looking for the meaning of life or wondering whether there is a light at the end of the proverbial tunnel and for the weak looking for strength, and those living a life of confusion I can tell you now, emphatically and in complete honesty, that there are answers to all your conundrums, there is strength, there is light at the end of even the longest tunnel and there is a meaning to life but it isn't just going to drop in to your lap, you have to search and fight for it.

Socially be nice, make as many friends and help as many people as you possibly can, suppress the ego and control all negative emotions. Privately, find and embrace adversity, through this you will develop tremendous mental strength, this being the key to the universe, with the backing of a strong mind there is nothing . . . nothing that cannot be attained. If there is no adversity there is no advance, also there is nothing like a little adversity to make you appreciate the finer things in life. If you want to become a leader of men you first have to become a leader of the 'self'.

Other books from Summersdale:

Watch My Back - *A Bouncer's Story*
(Prequel to *Bouncer*) by Geoff Thompson
"I read it in one go and couldn't put it down" Terry Christian, *The Word*
ISBN 1 873475 03 9 Hardback, 176pp, £12.99

Real Self Defence
Techniques, plus unique interviews with muggers and with their victims.
ISBN 1 873475 16 0 Paperback, 176pp, £12.99

Real Grappling
ISBN 1 873475 21 7 Paperback, 180pp, £12.99

Real Punching
ISBN 1 873475 26 8 Paperback, 176pp, £12.99

Real Kicking
ISBN 1 873475 31 4 Paperback, 176pp, £12.99

The Pavement Arena
Adapting combat martial arts to self defence in the 'street'.
ISBN 1 873475 11 X Paperback, 128pp, £9.95

The Student Grub Guide
Favourite easy recipes from around the world.
ISBN 1 873475 05 5 Paperback, 160pp, £4.95

Don't Lean Out of the Window! *Surviving Europe on a Train*
(Inter Rail travelogue - "Marvellous" Stephen Fry)
ISBN 1 873475 30 6 Paperback, 208pp, £4.95

From Horizontal To Vertical
Working with paralysed people in Bangladesh
Foreword by the BBC's Mark Tully.
ISBN 1 873475 01 2 Paperback, 154pp, £9.95

The Busker's Guide To Europe
How to make a fortune from your talents.
ISBN 1 873475 00 4 Paperback, 120pp, £5.95

Classic Love Poems
The perfect gift for a loved one.
ISBN 1 873475 50 0 Hardback, 176pp, £9.99

How To Chat-Up Women
A guide to forming relationships.
ISBN 1 873475 20 9 Paperback, 160pp, £6.99

These titles are available through all good bookshops. If ordering through a bookshop, please give the bookseller the title and the ISBN number. In case of difficulty, these books are available direct from the publisher. Send a cheque or postal order payable to Summersdale Publishers, and add £1.00 for postage and packaging. Our address is:

Summersdale Publishers
PO Box 49
Chichester
PO19 2FJ

Allow up to 28 days for delivery.
Prices valid until 31.12.95
After this date, write for latest prices.